PRAISE FOR
Heart of a Coach™

Besides the Bible, what could be a better tool for coaches who want to
be Christ followers than the blueprints, stories and experiences of fellow
coaches from around our country who seek to follow His will?
Heart of a Coach is a tool that will help us live in the sports arena in the
ways that God commands us to live in His kingdom.

JANE ALBRIGHT
Head Women's Basketball Coach
Wichita State University

The profession of coaching is one of the most powerful ministries in
our nation. Coaches of significance train athletes to become men and
women of significance. No matter where you are in your coaching career,
you will find *Heart of the Coach* inspiring and rewarding. This book is
a must-read for those who have chosen to work with young people.

BRUCE BROWN
Veteran Coach and Director of Proactive Coaching
NAIA Champions of Character Presenter

Heart of a Coach is a resource that will prove extremely valuable
in helping coaches maintain a balanced life. These devotionals will
motivate coaches to compete and to coach in a way that will
honor God and strengthen their character.

KEITH MADISON
Former Baseball Coach
University of Kentucky

Coaches always have a game plan. *Heart of a Coach* is an
exciting life plan that will inspire you in new ways as you
continue to read God's Word, think His thoughts and experience
His love. Believe me, this book is a winner.

FROSTY WESTERING
College Football Hall of Fame Coach
Retired Football Coach
Pacific Lutheran University

THE FCA COACH'S DEVOTIONAL

HEART
OF A
COACH™

Regal

From Gospel Light
Ventura, California, U.S.A.

PUBLISHED BY REGAL BOOKS
FROM GOSPEL LIGHT
VENTURA, CALIFORNIA, U.S.A.
Regal PRINTED IN THE U.S.A.

Regal Books is a ministry of Gospel Light, a Christian publisher dedicated to serving the local church. We believe God's vision for Gospel Light is to provide church leaders with biblical, user-friendly materials that will help them evangelize, disciple and minister to children, youth and families.

It is our prayer that this Regal book will help you discover biblical truth for your own life and help you meet the needs of others. May God richly bless you.

For a free catalog of resources from Regal Books/Gospel Light, please call your Christian supplier or contact us at 1-800-4-GOSPEL *or* www.regalbooks.com.

Library of Congress Cataloging-in-Publication Data
Heart of a coach / Fellowship of Christian Athletes.
    p. cm.
  ISBN 0-8307-3851-7 (trade paper)
  1. Devotional literature. 2. Sports—Religious aspects—Christianity. I. Fellowship of Christian Athletes.
  BV4801.H385 2005
  242'.68—dc22   2005029028

2   3   4   5   6   7   8   9   10   /   10   09   08   07   06

Rights for publishing this book in other languages are contracted by Gospel Light Worldwide, the international nonprofit ministry of Gospel Light. Gospel Light Worldwide also provides publishing and technical assistance to international publishers dedicated to producing Sunday School and Vacation Bible School curricula and books in the languages of the world. For additional information, visit www.gospellightworldwide.org; write to Gospel Light Worldwide, P.O. Box 3875, Ventura, CA 93006; or send an e-mail to info@gospel lightworldwide.org.

Contents

Foreword 12
John Wooden

Introduction 14
Les Steckel

New Beginnings 15
Ish Smith

Making a Contribution 16
Les Steckel

Pick Me! Pick Me! 18
Jere Johnson

Pregame Jitters 19
Michael Hill

Would You Rather? 21
Dan Britton

The Real Teacher 22
Jenny Johnson

Start Today 24
Jere Johnson

P.U.S.H. 25
Kathy Malone

Forget the Past 27
Chip Mehaffey

Patience 28
Wayne Morrow

The Plan 30
Michael Hill

You Can't Tell a Ball by Its Cover 31
Ish Smith

Priorities 33
Al Schierbaum

The Ultimate Goal 34
Michael Hill

Your Focus 36
Scott Wade

A New Way 37
Michael Wiggins

Commitment 39
Charles Gee

The Right Choice 40
Amy Walz

The Coaching Field . . . Our Mission Field 42
Sue Ramsey

Dreams 43
Roger Lipe

The Calling 45
Roger Lipe

No Knick Knocking 46
Kathy Malone

Measuring the Heart 48
Charles Gee

No Fear 49
Eileen F. Sommi

Encouragement 51
Bill Burnett

Confidence Building 52
Joel Schuldheisz

Choosing Sides 54
Les Steckel

First Response 55
Lisa Fisher

The Right Spot 57
Michael Wiggins

Smack 58
Jere Johnson

Exit the Roller Coaster 60
Chanda Husser Rigby

BIG GOD, Little Me 61
Scott Jackson

How Big Is Your Jesus? 63
Ken Kladnik

The Eternal Purpose 64
Michael Hill

A New Heart 66
Lisa Phillips

Self-Sacrifice 67
Donna Miller

Think Before You Speak 69
Jere Johnson

Following the Rules 70
Michael Hill

Sore Loser 72
Michael Wiggins

Troubled? 73
Clay Elliot

Nibbled to Death 75
Michael Wiggins

God's Grace 76
Danny Burns

God and the Apple 78
Laura Crawford

Know the Source 79
Michael Wiggins

Talk Is Cheap 81
Jere Johnson

God's Fearless Warrior 82
Jim Shapiro

C'mon, Blue! 84
John Ausmus

Mourning into Dancing 85
Josh Carter

In Joy 87
Lisa Phillips

Our Identity in Christ 88
Cheryl Baird

Devotion: A Way of Life 90
Al Schierbaum

You Are What You Think 91
Kathie Woods

Looking Forward 93
Jo Kadlecek

Some Winning Advice . . . Guaranteed 94
Clay Elliot

The Challenge of Coaching 96
Jere Johnson

Cheerleaders or Critics 97
Jim Faulk

H.O.T. Communication 99
Les Steckel

Little Things 100
Jere Johnson

Practice, Practice! 102
Clay Elliot

The Power of Fear 103
Bill Burnett

Weaknesses Lead to Strength 105
Cheryl Baird

Time-Out 106
Donalyn Knight

No "I" in Team 108
Josh Carter

Big Me, Little Team 109
Eileen F. Sommi

The Squeeze 111
Jere Johnson

Pressure Release 112
Debbie Haliday

The Voice of Truth 114
Jere Johnson

Doing the Right Thing 115
Michael Wiggins

Do the Deal, No Matter How You Feel 117
Jenny Burgins

Making Courageous Choices 118
Larry Kerr

Test Yourself 120
Josh Carter

No Excuses 121
Ken Kladnik

Help! 123
Kathy Malone

I'm Tired . . . He's Not 124
Cheryl Baird

Process over Product 126
Toby C. Schwartz

Focus 127
Bryan Wells

Recharging 129
Susan Johnson

Holding On 130
Alvin Cheng

The Coaching Tree 132
Jere Johnson

The Priceless Gift of Serving 133
Dan Britton

Blue Streaks 135
Brad Holloway

Off-Season Work 136
Jere Johnson

Lasting Leadership 138
Jere Johnson

The Power of Joy 139
Bill Burnett

What Will You Be Remembered For? 141
Rex Stump

Consumed by a Desire to Serve 142
Dan Britton

God's Game Plan 144
Jere Johnson

Free to Be Our Best 145
Phil Jones

Thankfulness: An Attitude of Gratitude 147
Al Schierbaum

True Success 148
Victor Santa Cruz

Endnotes 150

Thanks 151

Contributors 152

Impacting the World Through Sports 159

FCA Competitor's Creed 160

FCA Coach's Mandate 161

Good Reminders

I have supported the Fellowship of Christian Athletes almost from its beginning. Through the ensuing years, I have attended and spoken at many FCA meetings—including the Key to Life Award Banquet—and my children and grandchildren have enjoyed going to FCA camps.

One year, I heard a minister named Bob Menielly speak at an FCA event at Estes Park. He is the person who first gave me a poem titled *God's Hall of Fame*. I memorized that poem and have referred to it many times through the years.

In 1964, my UCLA team won our first NCAA men's basketball championship. The final game was in Kansas City, Missouri. In those days, it was played on a Saturday, not on a Monday as it is today. We capped an undefeated season by beating Duke 98-83. I was feeling pretty good.

The next day was Easter Sunday, and I wanted to hear Bob Menielly speak at his church, which was near Kansas City. With my assistant coach and our wives, we headed off to the service. As we walked from the car to the sanctuary, a pigeon scouted out our little group, no doubt noticing that we were wearing our Sunday bests, including fashionable hats. The pigeon's aim was perfect. Plop, his little gift of humility landed right on top of my new hat. Here my team had just won the national championship and I was feeling very pleased with life, and along came the pigeon. I think he was a messenger, perhaps from God. From that point on, I always kept in mind my proper place, even after winning championships.

I do not tell this story often, but I think that it is a good reminder for anyone who is a coach. After all, it is our humility that enables us to control our emotions during the good times and the bad. It is good to have other reminders, too. Since 1942, I have carried a small cross in my pocket. No, it is not a good luck charm; rather, it is a reminder. Whenever I place my hand in my pocket and grasp that cross, my proper perspective returns. If we are at peace with Christ, we will not be so wrapped up with ourselves, nor will we be so vulnerable to the ups and downs of a particular practice, game or season. We will build a shelter for eternity rather than an E-Z Up® canopy that we fold up after each game.

Every day, I read the Bible. I also read books, poems and devotions—most anything of value. Each night, when I go to bed, I recite poetry until I fall asleep. What I read and what I recite serve as reminders, like the pigeon and the cross. Words of inspiration remind me that real success does not come from the number of championships a coach wins, the size of his or her contract, or the level of his or her fame. Words of reassurance remind me that success only comes when, at the end of the day, we have peace of mind and peace with God.

Before you is a wonderful book of devotional readings. I encourage you to read one each day. Let them remind, teach and speak to you about character, truth and all that really matters in the heart of a coach. Use them as you seek to be an example to your players and a keeper of the faith. Let them help bring you the peace of mind that comes when you have peace with God.

John Wooden
Head Basketball Coach, 1948-1975
UCLA

Teammates:

For over 50 years, FCA has been privileged to minister to coaches by encouraging and equipping them to know and serve the Master Coach, Jesus Christ. One of our priorities is to develop resources to engage coaches and help them integrate their faith and sport. We want them to see that coaching is ministry.

Coaching is all about relationships. Whether it's a player, a fellow coach or our family, the only way to get to know a person is to spend time with him or her. These 90 devotionals are designed to help you develop a focused time with God. They are written from a coach's point of view and include pertinent verses from the Bible to help you gain an understanding of God's perspective on issues you face in your daily life. Our hope is that this book will motivate you to have a consistent training time and read God's playbook to deepen your understanding of His Word.

As a coach, you have been given a tremendous platform to influence others. Our prayer is that God will use this tool to transform your life as a coach so that you can make an eternal impact, not only in your life, but also in the lives of others.

Godspeed,

Les Steckel
FCA President/CEO

In the beginning God created the heavens and
the earth. Now the earth was formless and empty,
darkness covered the surface of the watery depths,
and the Spirit of God was hovering over
the surface of the waters.

GENESIS 1:1-2

"In the beginning, God created . . ." These are familiar words to most who know that this verse refers to the creation of the world. Sometimes, in a humorous vein, those of us who love baseball will try to identify the Creator with our game by quoting the above verse as "In the big inning . . ."

I believe that we can learn an important lesson from those first five words in the Bible—one that relates more to those of us who live on the earth than it does to the earth itself. God did not stop creating thousands of years ago when He put in His week's work and then rested on the seventh day. No, the good news of the gospel is that God wants to continue to create in our lives, and, for us, today can be a *new beginning*.

As I reflect on my years of coaching, I can vividly remember the euphoria that was always present each year when I would go to the equipment room and bring out the bats, balls, gloves, spikes and uniforms. For all of us who claim Christ as Lord of our lives, we have reason to experience that same euphoria.

Yes, there is a "beginning" when we accept Christ as our Savior—maybe it could even be referred to as "the Big Inning." But God has many more beginnings in store for our lives. He wants to re-create us for new challenges and to empower us anew for responsibilities that are headed our way. When we fall, He anxiously awaits our invitation so that He might provide a new beginning in our lives.
—*Ish Smith*

1. Is it time for a new beginning in your life?

2. Are you living out a chapter or season in your life that needs to come to an end?

3. What are some "new beginnings" that you would like to see in your life?

Scripture: Ezekiel 36:26; John 1:1-14; 2 Corinthians 5:16-21

Prayer: *Lord, begin in me a new work so that I may honor You in all that I do. Amen.*

Making a Contribution

Then He said to them all, "If anyone wants to come with Me, he must deny himself, take up his cross daily, and follow Me."

LUKE 9:23

In a recent survey, managers and employees were asked what aspects of their job were most important to them. The results uncovered that while the managers focused on things such as job security and benefits, the employees simply wanted to know that they were contributing—that what they were doing made a difference.

What is the first thing that we as athletes or coaches look for when we see the new team photograph? Ourselves, right? We all do. We are naturally selfish beings. Coaches might say, "There's no 'I' in 'team,'" but no matter how many times we reiterate this point, the "I" is always a problem. We fight a daily battle with selfishness, which of course affects how we contribute not only to our teams or businesses but also to our families—and even to our relationship with Christ.

Though it is human nature to be self-centered, it is also in our nature to genuinely want to make a contribution. However, the two are often in conflict with each other. This is why we should check our motives whenever we are in a position to give. Do we want to contribute based on the "I" or on the "team"? Is it about the "me" or about the "we"?

Jesus Christ was the only human who did not yield to selfish tendencies. He offered the greatest contribution humanity has ever known: the sacrifice of His life for our sins! In order to make a powerful impact for Christ and contribute our gifts to building His kingdom, we are called to follow His selfless example. Through His power in us, we can live out Jesus' words in Luke 9:23, denying ourselves in following Him. When we do, it will undoubtedly lead to the most significant contribution we'll ever make! —*Les Steckel*

1. Are your contributions for your sake, or for Christ and His Body of believers?

2. When has another person put your needs before his or her own? How did you feel?

3. Are you on the side of the "me" or of the "we"?

Scripture: Proverbs 11:2; John 3:27-30; Philippians 2:1-4; 1 Peter 5:1-7

Prayer: *Lord, I pray that You would increase in me as I decrease! Amen.*

> Jesus offered the greatest contribution humanity has ever known: the sacrifice of His life for our sins!

Pick Me! Pick Me!

> Accept my instruction instead of silver, and knowledge rather than pure gold. For wisdom is better than precious stones, and nothing desirable can compare with it.
>
> PROVERBS 8:10-11

Coaches often travel the country recruiting future players, selling their programs and enticing future stars to choose to attend their schools. Blue-chip recruits are in high demand, and every coach is inwardly yelling, "Pick me! Pick me!"

In the same way, wisdom calls out to us and pleads her case about why we should pick her. Choosing wisdom is invaluable; it is better than solid gold or pure silver. It is better than the best thing we could ever want. Why? As the writer says in Proverbs 8:34-35, whoever finds wisdom finds happiness and life and obtains favor from the Lord.

So what is wisdom? How do we recognize it or nurture it? We find wisdom in the person of Jesus Christ, who lived a sinless life on Earth yet was with the Father in the beginning of creation when wisdom was formed (see Proverbs 8:22). Hebrews 1:2-3 tells us that God "has spoken to us by His Son, whom He has appointed heir of all things and *through whom* He made the universe. He is the radiance of His glory, the exact expression of His nature, and He sustains all things by His powerful word" (emphasis added). In Jesus, we discover the exact representation of God's sustaining wisdom. And when we live in Him, we grow in the knowledge and wisdom that guides our lives. With Him, there is health, peace and life.

As we act out wise choices and decisions based on our relationship with Christ, we will experience the rich harvest that righteous living brings! Wisdom is calling out to us, "Pick me! Pick me!" When we do, we will never be disappointed! —*Jere Johnson*

1. How have you chosen wisdom in different situations? Foolishness?

2. What do you consider to be authentic godly wisdom?

3. How can you start living in the wisdom that comes from Christ?

Scripture: Proverbs 8; Luke 2:52; 1 Corinthians 1:25; James 1:5; 3:13-18

Prayer: *Eternal God, guide me this day with the mind of Christ, and protect my heart with the grace that wisdom brings. Amen.*

Pregame Jitters

Who of you by worrying can add a single hour to his life? Since you cannot do this very little thing, why do you worry about the rest?
LUKE 12:25, *NIV*

We've all been there. It's only a few minutes before "show time." We hear the band playing to get the crowd excited for the game. We look around the locker room and see our players trying to get into the "zone." We've worked hard to get them prepared, but something isn't clicking.

The team has the pregame jitters! Maybe they think they aren't as talented as their opponent. Maybe they lack confidence in the game plan. Maybe they don't want to look bad in front of all those fans and media. Or maybe they are nervous that they won't live up to their own expectations. Whatever the reason, the result is the same: worry and a lack of focus.

All of us who have competed know that feeling in the pit of our stomach. Sometimes we're not even sure whether it's fear or excitement, whether we should scream or cry. The men around Jesus had the jitters, too. Like us, they had anxiety about everyday life. But in Luke 12:22-26, Jesus put the "game" in proper perspective for his followers. He told them that if God takes care of the needs of the ravens, He would also take care of those who are worth much more to Him than the birds.

Jesus went on to remind His disciples that worrying would add nothing to their lives. In other words, it was wasted energy. Then, in case they were still tempted to worry, He went a step further to prove God's faithfulness by willingly taking their sins to the cross! If Jesus reminded His disciples of God's provision in spite of their jitters and proved it with His life, death and resurrection, why should we worry about our game? —*Michael Hill*

1. What situations make you nervous?

2. How do you overcome the jitters?

3. What does Jesus invite us to do when we feel nervous?

Scripture: Matthew 6:25-34; 8:23-27; Luke 12:22-34; 1 Peter 5:7

Prayer: *Lord, please forgive me for worrying and for forgetting how much You love me and care for me. I pray that You would turn my fears into faith as I remember Your provision in Jesus Christ. Amen.*

> Whatever the reason, the result
> of pregame jitters is the same:
> worry and a lack of focus.

If anyone wants to be first, he must
be last of all and servant of all.
MARK 9:35

Our family plays a great game at the dinner table called "Would You Rather." We ask the question "Would you rather . . . ?" so that our children have to make a decision, such as, "Would you rather win a World Series or a Super Bowl?"

Last night, I decided to ask my three kids the following question: "Would you rather be a great leader or a great servant?" I barely had time to finish the question before my 10-year-old daughter replied, "Dad, they're the same thing. If you serve someone, you are showing and teaching someone what Jesus would do!" Wow! After picking myself up off the ground, I realized that she had nailed it. In God's eyes, a great servant is always a great leader, but a great leader is not necessarily a great servant.

In the arena of competition, whether playing or coaching, we need to understand what it means to be a great servant. Being a great servant in the athletic world does not mean serving others in order to become a great leader; rather, it means sacrificing and dying to self. I don't know about you, but for me this is hard. It means putting the interests of my teammates first—both on and off the field. It means having an attitude like Christ's as I place their needs before my own. As competitors, we need to realize that this battle to lead or to serve rages every day.

So, if I had asked you "Would you rather be a great leader or a great servant?" what would have been your answer? —*Dan Britton*

1. Why do people today elevate leaders so much?
   Can the same be said of servants?
   Why or why not?

2. Name one of the greatest modern-day servants. Name a servant in the world of sports. What makes them special?

3. What is one way that you can put the needs of your athletes or fellow coaches before your own?

Scripture: Matthew 20:23-28; 23:11-12; Philippians 2:1-11

Prayer: *Lord, teach me today to put the needs of others before my own. Make me a great servant as I seek to follow in Your footsteps. Amen.*

The Real Teachers

Therefore, God's chosen ones, holy and loved, put on heartfelt compassion, kindness, humility, gentleness, and patience.
COLOSSIANS 3:12

My very first day of coaching high school girls' tennis fell on a hot August afternoon. As our practice was about to end, the only thing left was our distance run. I had my stopwatch ready to call out the time of each player as she finished. I knew this was going to be tough that first day. Nobody was in great shape at the end of the summer—too many afternoons spent lying on the couch in air-conditioned comfort.

When the first runner crossed the finish line, I called out her time. Immediately, she turned around to see how far back the other players were and saw one young player far behind everyone else. Without hesitating, she sprinted back to that last runner and began to run alongside her for the last leg. Our fastest runner did not want anyone to have to finish last or alone!

I was amazed. I remembered my own days playing high school basketball. If I had finished my laps before anyone else, I know that I wouldn't have been thinking about anyone else. Instead, I would have found a nice cool spot on the gym floor and plopped down to rest. But on this first day of coaching high school tennis, I suddenly realized that I was going to be *learning* a lot more than I'd be *teaching*.

Through that young player, God taught me a lesson about kindness and sensitivity—a lesson that I've never forgotten. Just as Jesus Christ amazed the local leaders with His deeds and words, God used the unexpected to change me in a way that I could never have imagined. He still does! —*Jenny Johnson*

1. What lessons have you learned from your players?

2. How has God used the unexpected to teach you something that He wanted you to learn?

3. Would others view you as having compassion, kindness, humility, gentleness and patience, of being as Christlike as the young player who came alongside the last runner?

Scripture: Proverbs 20:11; Ephesians 4:31-32; 1 John 3:8-20

Prayer: *Thank You, almighty God, for coming to Earth in the Person of Jesus to "run" beside me in some amazing ways! Amen.*

> Whatever you did for one of the least of these brothers of Mine, you did for Me.
>
> Matthew 25:40

Start Today

But if it doesn't please you to worship the Lord, choose for yourselves today the one you will worship: the gods your fathers worshiped beyond the Euphrates River, or the gods of the Amorites in whose land you are living.

JOSHUA 24:15

For a goal-oriented society, we sure procrastinate a lot. It seems like we are always putting something off, believing that it can wait until we have time to get to it later. However, whether we're self-serving, unwilling, or simply naïve, we often forget that we are not guaranteed tomorrow. *Today* is the day to make necessary changes in our lives. But we are creatures of habit, and the bad habits, wrong choices or mistakes that we make can affect every aspect of our lives—athletic, social and spiritual.

Because Joshua understood human nature, he challenged his people to choose "today" whom they would serve. He knew that he and his family would choose to worship the Lord. He also knew that life might not always be easy. Still, Joshua understood that God was trustworthy—focusing on the Lord would be his only hope when struggles came.

Joshua's example reminds us that we need a Savior to rescue us from . . . ourselves! Thankfully, Jesus came to Earth as God-made Man and proclaimed that today is the day of salvation (see 2 Corinthians 6:2). He provided a way for us to turn from our bad decisions and wrong paths and be led out of darkness and despair. Through Christ's death on the cross, we are invited to worship the Lord so that He can begin to change us. We don't need to change first; we only need to come to Him.

Just as He gave all, so does He want all of us. He does not promise us tomorrow, but He does promise to be with us (see Matthew 28:20). If we choose today to worship Him, we will become more like Him and see His image reflected in our own. —*Jere Johnson*

1. Do you need a fresh start? A new beginning?

2. What habits do you need to bring to the Cross in order to grow closer to God?

3. How can you live a life of worship to God—*today*?

Scripture: Joshua 24:14-15; Psalm 118:24; James 4:13-17

Prayer: *Almighty God, draw me near to You today and put a song of worship in my heart all day long! Amen.*

P.U.S.H.

With every prayer and request, pray at all times in the Spirit, and stay alert in this, with all perseverance and intercession for all the saints.

EPHESIANS 6:18

I will never forget watching Reggie Miller score 8 points in the last 32 seconds of a 1995 Eastern Conference NBA playoff game in Madison Square Garden. Miller's never-say-die heroics in the closing seconds gave the Indiana Pacers a thrilling 2-point victory over the New York Knicks. Throughout his 18-year career with the Pacers, Miller was the picture of persistence. He didn't make every clutch shot he took, but he never stopped shooting them.

In an interview following his final NBA game, he summed up his career by saying:

> I showed up each and every day to play. I played in 80 percent of my games, maybe more. I played hurt. You never knew

when someone was coming to an Indiana Pacers basketball game for the first time . . . I always wanted them to remember that they had an enjoyable experience when they saw the Indiana Pacers play.[1]

Just as Miller modeled persistence, so too do good coaches. Would a good coach ever tell her team to give up just because they were down by 10 points at halftime? Never! She would encourage her players to fight to the end, no matter how things looked at any point during the game. Athletes and coaches understand, perhaps better than most, the need for persistence when it comes to competition.

Can the same be said of us when it comes to prayer? Have we talked with God regularly and honestly? Have we prayed and persisted, even when it didn't look like victory was possible? Jesus said, "Keep searching, and you will find" (Matthew 7:7). We are to continue to come before God with our requests, even when it feels like nothing is happening.

I've seen popular bracelets with the acronym P.U.S.H. stitched on them: "Pray Until Something Happens." What a great reminder that we should never give up when it comes to making our requests known to a God who loves us and gave His Son that we might find Him! —*Kathy Malone*

1. Do you have an attitude of perseverance when it comes to prayer?

2. What prayer have you given up on?

3. What is keeping you from picking up that prayer and bringing it back to the Father?

Scripture: Luke 18:1; Colossians 4:2; Philippians 4:6

Prayer: *Lord, forgive me for giving up so easily when it comes to prayer. Teach me to persevere in prayer as Your unseen hand works in ways I can't see or understand. Draw me into Your presence today through Your Holy Spirit. Amen.*

> Brothers, I do not consider myself to have
> taken hold of it. But one thing I do: forgetting what
> is behind and reaching forward to what is ahead,
> I pursue as my goal the prize promised by God's
> heavenly call in Christ Jesus.
>
> PHILIPPIANS 3:13-14

As a high school basketball coach, I often notice that my players are influenced by the past. After a winning streak, they sometimes begin to believe that they are better than they actually are. Such overconfidence can lead to deflating defeats. Yet the same happens after a losing streak; the team loses confidence in their abilities.

To avoid either of these, many coaches remind their teams to stay focused. John Wooden always said, "Don't let your highs be too high, or your lows too low." In our program, we remind our players to focus on what lies ahead rather than on the past. After each game, we say, "The season starts tomorrow." This helps us remember what we, as a team, can become.

As Christians, we're sometimes too hard on ourselves when we reflect upon our past sins. Satan can use this to try to make us feel unworthy of God and His kingdom. The truth is, though, we are unworthy! That's the good news of the gospel: We are all sinners, but we are not unlovable. Salvation is never something we earn, which is why Jesus paid the ultimate price on the cross so that we could be saved!

Paul said in Philippians to forget "what is behind" and reach "forward to what is ahead." God can still do great things with us regardless of our past. He says to each of us, "Your Christian life begins today *because* I love you!" In return, the greatest gift we can offer others is the good news that God looks beyond our past to give us grace for the future—if only we'll receive it! —*Chip Mehaffey*

1. What from your past do you need to let go?

2. What changes does God want to make in you?

3. How can you grow in His love?

Scripture: 2 Corinthians 4:7-9; 1 John 2:12

Prayer: *I confess, Lord Jesus, that I often allow my sin to take me away from You. Thank You that You forgive me and love me, and that You have redeemed me by Your death and resurrection so that I can move forward with You! Amen.*

Patience

But endurance must do its complete work, so that you may be mature and complete, lacking nothing.

JAMES 1:4

In our culture, patience is becoming less and less common. We're an "instant gratification" society, and when things don't go according to our timetable or plans, we get frustrated and sometimes angry. How many times have coaches lost their temper when an athlete didn't make the right play or the right decision?

Biblical patience is a much-needed virtue these days, and it is certainly a reflection of where we are in our Christian walk. For instance, one of the best-known "athletic" verses in the Bible is Isaiah 40:31: "But those who trust in the Lord will renew their strength; they will soar on wings like eagles; they will run and not grow weary; they will walk and not faint." The key word in the truth of this promise is "trust." We know that we should trust, or wait on the Lord, by serving Him, much like a waiter in a restaurant serves a table, though that's not always easy. It also means that we need to be patient as we wait for God's leading in every aspect of life.

Merrill Unger defined patience as

> That calm and unruffled temper with which the good man bears the evils of life, whether they proceed from persons or things. It also manifests itself in a sweet submission to the providential appointments of God and fortitude in the presence of the duties and conflicts of life.

How do we develop such godly patience? By looking to Jesus Christ, who not only exhibited great patience and kindness with His disciples but who also continues to show us the ultimate patience.

Instead of receiving the punishment we deserve for our sins, He gives us forgiveness by taking our sins to the cross. Instead of condemnation, He gives us grace, over and over again. His patience *with* us creates patience *in* us—patience we can then exhibit in our relationships with our athletes, families, coworkers and friends!
—*Wayne Morrow*

1. What things in your life try your patience?

2. How do you react when things don't go according to your plans?

3. How can you demonstrate better patience with your players, friends and family?

Scripture: Proverbs 16:32; 19:11; Romans 15:4-5; 2 Timothy 4:1-5

Prayer: *Merciful God, help me to wait on You today as You create in me an eternal perspective. Amen.*

The Plan

"For I know the plans I have for you"—[this is] the Lord's declaration—plans for [your] welfare, not for disaster, to give you a future and a hope. You will call to Me and come and pray to Me, and I will listen to you.

JEREMIAH 29:11-12

As a football coach at both the college and high school levels, it seemed like I was always making plans. I would spend hours watching films and charting out an opposing team's offensive tendencies. I would then try to come up with a strategy to stop their offense. When the season was over, I would start preparing to improve our team in the off-season. Whether it was coming up with a plan to recruit the best high school players or organizing an off-season weight-lifting program, it seemed as if I was always planning for something.

The big thing with plans is that we have to trust they will work. We might start out with a goal, come up with a strategy to attain it, and then trust that our hard work will pay off. But there is one catch: No plan of ours ever works exactly the way it did on paper! Only one plan has ever come out as it was intended, and that is God's!

The prophet Jeremiah wrote that God's declaration to us involves a plan for our welfare, to care for us and to provide for us the gift of hope each day of our earthly lives. In the person of Jesus Christ, God's promise has been fulfilled! For it is through the gospel of Christ—that is, the good news of His life, death and resurrection—that we are saved from disaster and given a future that is anchored in His marvelous love. His plan has always been to bring us into a personal relationship with Him—not to have us fulfill a set of goals and strategies! By seeking God's presence, we can always be confident that He has a plan. —*Michael Hill*

1. How are you actively seeking God in your life?

2. In what area of your life are you having problems trusting God?

3. What steps can you take to trust in God's purposes for your life?

Scripture: Joshua 1:9; Psalm 20:7; Proverbs 3:5; 16:20; 1 Peter 2:6

Prayer: *Lord, today when I'm tempted to pursue my own strategy or agenda, draw me close to You so that your Kingdom purposes might be fulfilled in me! Amen.*

You Can't Tell a Ball by Its Cover

Woe to you, scribes and Pharisees, hypocrites!
You clean the outside of the cup and dish, but inside
they are full of greed and self-indulgence!
MATTHEW 23:25

There are two sayings that I have heard hundreds of times in my life. One is "You can't tell a book by its cover," and the other is an advertising statement that assures us "It's what's up front that counts." I would like to take a little liberty with those two statements and apply them to the world of sports. I think that anyone who has played baseball can attest to the fact that "You can't tell a baseball by its cover" and "It's what's inside that counts."

Go to your local sporting goods store and you can buy a baseball for about $3.00 or you can pay almost $10.00 for a baseball. On the outside, both of those baseballs will look very much alike—both will have "official" marked on their cover, and both may even have exactly the same number of stitches. But baseball coaches and players know that the core of these baseballs and the material used in winding the inside of each of these baseballs will be very different. You won't be able to tell by looking on the outside or at the cover, but once you look inside the ball, the truth will be made clear.

What is true for a baseball is true for a coach. The true test of a coach isn't what he or she looks like, but what is inside. Those intangibles often separate the great coaches from the average ones. As a coach, you can make an impression with how you look. But over a season, and particularly when the going gets tough, the truth of what you are made of will come out. —*Ish Smith*

1. How do you react under the pressure of tough times?

2. Do your players know you as one who walks the talk?

3. How would game officials describe you as a coach?

Scripture: 1 Samuel 16:1-7; 17:31-37; 17:41-47

Prayer: *Lord, I want to be a coach of whom You can be proud. I want my players, opponents, fans and sports officials to see me as one who lives a consistent Christian life and shows Your love to all with whom I come in contact. Amen.*

Do not look at his appearance or his stature, because I have rejected him. Man does not see what the Lord sees, for man sees what is visible, but the Lord sees the heart.

1 Samuel 16:7

Watch out and be on guard against all greed, because one's life is not in the abundance of his possessions.

LUKE 12:15

At the beginning of every football season, Coach Tom Landry would give his players his priorities: God, family and football, in that order. By keeping these priorities, he avoided the madness and chaos that often consume a coach's life.

These priorities provide great wisdom for us as we seek balance in our lives. When we keep first things first, we honor God and others around us, which helps us avoid relational destruction. Sadly, though, many coaches become "life losers" because they put their sport first and everything else second. They measure their self-worth by what they accomplish on the athletic field and by the wins they attain. In the process, everything else suffers. Their families fall apart, and they feel empty because their soul is not being nourished by a relationship with God.

Jesus warns us against getting caught in this web of deception. In fact, He says that at the heart of this "accomplishment complex" is personal greed. For coaches, this translates as an attitude in which the only ambition is winning. But when we approach life in this way, everyone becomes a pawn in our game. If they can't produce for us, they become disposable. Family responsibilities become a nuisance, players who can't perform have little worth, and coaches who can't keep up are second-class citizens. This attitude produces a no-win season in God's eyes because it puts another god before the one true God, Jesus Christ.

Putting Jesus first means keeping Him at the center of all we do, remembering that we were at the center of why He came to Earth! By keeping Him first, we can't help but pursue excellence for His sake and keep our careers in proper perspective. Jesus wants to be our sole ambition—and when He is, our coaching will be better than ever!
—*Al Schierbaum*

1. How does knowing that God loves you unconditionally shape your perspective?

2. What were Jesus' priorities?

3. What changes in your life can you make to reflect God's priorities?

Scripture: Psalm 127:1-5; Ecclesiastes 2:24-25; Matthew 22:37-39; Galatians 5:16-26

Prayer: *Gracious Father, turn my eyes away from the empty ambitions of this world so that I might see today the depths and riches of Your love in Christ Jesus!*

The Ultimate Goal

I want to know Christ and the power of his resurrection and the fellowship of sharing in his sufferings, becoming like him in his death.

PHILIPPIANS 3:10, *NIV*

As coaches, we challenge our players to set goals. If we were to look in their lockers or playbooks, we might find a list of personal expectations and team goals. Because they need to reinforce their goals once they set them, they often pick up paper and pen to write them down.

The great apostle Paul also had goals, one of which appears in his letter to the church at Philippi. Paul's goal was to know Jesus more. If we wrote this goal down on a list that we had for ourselves and for our players, what would be the result? Would that undefeated team look as daunting if we knew "the power of his resurrection"? Would the daily challenges of our jobs, the personal pains of failed relationships, or the real sorrows of daily tragedies seem as unendurable if we knew "the fellowship of sharing in his sufferings"?

Knowing Christ was Paul's goal because he had been delivered from the darkness of a terrible existence and brought into the light of God's forgiveness. He had encountered the risen Lord Jesus, the One who overlooked his tragic life and redeemed it with the price of His death on the cross. As a result, Paul could not help but want to know his Savior better!

That intense love for Jesus could be ours as well. If we set goals to improve our team's performance, why don't we also set goals to improve our relationship with Jesus Christ? And just like we do with our team goals, we can continually assess our progress by bringing them into the light of God's love and remembering His power at work within us! —*Michael Hill*

1. What are your goals?

2. How many of your goals include growing closer to God?

3. What can you do today to grow closer to God?

Scripture: Psalm 51; Acts 9:1-31; Philippians 1:27-29; 1 Timothy 1:12-17

Prayer: *Lord, draw me closer to You today I as walk through the doors that You have opened for me so that I might do Your work. Please help me to know Christ better and reflect His grace for Your sake. Amen.*

> If we wrote down "knowing Jesus more" as a goal for ourselves and our players, what would be the result?

> So we do not focus on what is seen,
> but on what is unseen; for what is seen is
> temporary, but what is unseen is eternal.
>
> 2 CORINTHIANS 4:18

I'll never forget the first day of football camp at the small college I attended. I'd come hoping to be a part of a winning program and perhaps even a national championship. Our head coach had scheduled a team meeting, and as he reviewed the goals, he pulled out the video of last year's national championship, a game that we'd lost. I expected him to share his strategy for how we could make it back to the national championship this year and win. Instead, he did something I will never forget: He threw the video to the ground, stomped it to bits and told us that if our only dream was to win a national championship, then we'd set our goals too low!

That season, I learned what my coach was talking about. We went undefeated and reached the championship game against the team that had beaten us the previous year. We lost in four overtimes, but that's not what the season had been all about. Through the influence of Christian coaches and players, 12 of my teammates made the decision to follow Christ. While most of us will forget that season's record, those decisions made during that season will have eternal significance!

As the apostle Paul wrote, rather than focusing on what is seen, our vision as Christians should be set on that which we cannot see. That is the faith we've been given through Jesus Christ, whose vision for God's kingdom was why He came to Earth. He clung to the hope of eternity with those He loved (us!) and it allowed Him to endure the most famous execution in all of human history. Jesus saw beyond this world and into the next! Just as our football coach taught us, our goals, too, should be on the highest level! —*Scott Wade*

1. What goals are you setting for your team?

2. How do you use your sport to build the character of your players?

3. What is your ultimate goal?

Scripture: Matthew 6:19-24; 1 Corinthians 1:24-27; Hebrews 12:1-2

Prayer: *Lord, enlighten the eyes of my heart that my vision may be for You and how we together can guide my team to a championship that lasts forever! Amen.*

A New Way

> For although I am free from all people,
> I have made myself a slave to all, in order
> to win more people.
>
> 1 CORINTHIANS 9:19

In the 1964 Tokyo Olympic Games, sprinter Bob Hayes tied the Olympic record on his way to winning the gold medal in the 100-meter dash. Just a few months later, Hayes was dashing past defensive backs as a wide receiver for the Dallas Cowboys.

It was a radical idea at the time: taking a world-class sprinter and turning him into a football player. Hayes's success altered defensive strategy and changed how football was played.

Coaches design drills to improve players' technique and help them gain strength and increase their speed. These improvements are typically made in small increments: A few more yards are gained with the driver; a few more pounds are added to a bench press a few tenths of a second are shaved off the time for a 40-yard dash.

Hours of work can go into making the smallest advance. But sometimes, an innovation occurs that radically redefines the way a sport is played, causing such a drastic change that teams and players are forced to adapt. They must trade in their wooden tennis racquets, move away from their wishbone offenses, or give up their steel bicycles. Those who refuse to adjust are defeated.

Christians must also acknowledge the power of innovation. While God is unchanging, the people who need Him are forever changing. Societies, cultures and tastes all change. As Christians, we must recognize this and alter the way we communicate God's message of love and forgiveness to others.

We must be creative in how we reach those who don't know about the work and grace of Jesus Christ. If we fail to be innovative in our presentation of God's message, the world will assume that the message is no longer relevant to their lives.

God wants us to bring others to Him. So let's explore new ways of spreading God's message of love and forgiveness. —*Michael Wiggins*

1. How did Jesus communicate with His disciples?

2. As the disciples grew in their faith, how did they change?

3. What adjustments is God asking you to make in your life plan?

Scripture: Matthew 5:43-48; Acts 10:11-13; 1 Corinthians 9:19-23

Prayer: *God, thank You that You never change. Lead me into new areas of growth for Your sake! Amen.*

Elisha left the oxen, ran to follow Elijah, and said, "Please let me kiss my father and mother, and then I will follow you." "Go on back," he replied, "for what have I done to you?" So he turned back from following him, took the team of oxen, and slaughtered them. With the oxen's wooden yoke and plow, he cooked the meat and gave it to the people, and they ate. Then he left, followed Elijah, and served him.

1 KINGS 19:19-21

Every year college coaches agonize over recruits, hoping that a star athlete will commit to signing with his or her team. But recruits can make a "soft" commitment to a school while they continue visiting other campuses. Though the definition of "commit" is "to bind" or "obligate" (which implies a definite decision), the meaning of this word has obviously been diluted in the world of college recruiting.

Commitment meant something totally different to Elisha. He was plowing in a field when Elijah found him, threw his cloak around him and pronounced him as his successor. Elisha responded by asking permission first to go home to prepare a farewell feast. He slaughtered the oxen, burned the plow to cook the meat and fed his people. Then he followed Elijah and became his servant. Elisha's response was hardly a "soft" commitment; he left no doubt that he was binding himself to Elijah.

In the same way, God became man in the person of Jesus Christ, leaving no doubt of His commitment to us. Through His sacrificial blood, He now invites us to an eternal feast with Him! Because of His amazing bond of love to us, He desires that we, too, live lives of firm—not soft—commitments in all that we do. That's not easy to do in a culture that encourages us to avoid commitments and wander off if a more attractive offer comes along. But God knows our hearts, and just as He did with Elisha, He provides the strength that we need to carry out our commitments for His sake. —*Charles Gee*

1. How does it affect you when a player displays an Elisha-like commitment?

2. To what or to whom are you committed?

3. How can you demonstrate commitment to God?

Scripture: Proverbs 20:25; Mark 10:29-31; Luke 9:57-62

Prayer: *Almighty God, I'm grateful that You sacrificed Your only Son out of a committed love for me. Empower me today to show the same devoted love to others! Amen.*

The Right Choice

As for me and my family, we will worship the Lord.
JOSHUA 24:15

What does it take to win the game? The answer to this question often dictates the primary philosophy that coaches use as the basis of their decisions. Under ever-increasing pressure to win, every coach and player has been encouraged to bend or break the rules. In the world of sports, why is it so difficult to discern what constitutes cheating?

In the 1999 Women's Soccer World Cup, U.S.A. goalkeeper Brianna Scurry stepped off her goal line to make the game-winning save on a penalty kick. While the rules allow a goalkeeper to move sideways along the line, he or she is not allowed to step forward until the ball is kicked. In the championship match that day, the referee did not rule against the save. It is still a point of contention whether the referee and the player made the right choice.

Making the right choice and acting with integrity become even more challenging when it appears that our competitors are not doing the same. How can our players be expected to compete against a team that practices extra days or uses ineligible players or illegal equipment?

As believers in Jesus Christ, God calls us to a higher standard, which He proved by sending His only Son to Earth so that we might come to Him. He desires that we act with integrity in every aspect of our life, including in our athletic competitions, but He did not leave us on our own to fulfill that call to live by His standards. He provided a way through a personal relationship in Christ. As coaches, we desire to win. Yet God does not want us to win the game at the cost of losing our integrity. —*Amy Walz*

1. What does it mean for you as a coach to serve the Lord with integrity?

2. As a coach, what actions help you make the right choice when confronted with a difficult decision?

3. How can you model biblical integrity to your players and colleagues?

Scripture: Psalm 37; Proverbs 24:10; Romans 12:21

Prayer: *Lord, I desire to serve You. Help me to make the right choices and encourage my players to do the same. Give me the strength to act with integrity, even when others choose not to. Allow me to stand firm in my decisions and rest in the peace and love only You provide. Amen.*

> For what does it benefit a man to gain the whole world yet lose his life?
> Mark 8:36

Shepherd God's flock among you, not overseeing
out of compulsion but freely, according to God's will;
not for the money but eagerly; not lording it over those
entrusted to you, but being examples to the flock.
And when the chief Shepherd appears, you will
receive the unfading crown of glory.

1 PETER 5:2-4

Competition is an obvious part of the coaching life, resulting in either winning or losing. But God's Word reminds us not to get so caught up in the results that we forget to take care of the flock—the athletes—who have been put under our watch.

Of course, we all want to win. Yet if we forget that we're really working toward an imperishable crown (as Paul writes in 1 Corinthians 9:25), then we've lost sight of why we're coaching in the first place. In other words, just as we live our lives to please the Good Shepherd, so too should we coach our players with the same goal. In the process, we'll serve as examples to the sheep.

The Lord has given us our "mission field," and He cares more about how we take care of the people He has entrusted to us than He does about our win-loss record. This is why Peter provides us with guidelines from the verses above on how to serve our athletes. We are to guide the flock (team) not by coercion or constraint, but willingly; not dishonorably, motivated by the advantages and profits, but eagerly and cheerfully; not with intimidation, but by being an example to them. And when the Chief Shepherd, Jesus Christ, appears again, we will win the unfading crown of glory!

This is our hope. Until then, God is able to help us accomplish our goal every day, through not only our words but also our actions, as He cares for our players through us! —*Sue Ramsey*

1. Does your coaching style reflect the shepherding characteristics described by Peter?

2. What creative ways could you care for your athletes and thereby please Christ?

3. When you honestly assess your motives, do you seek advantages and profits, or do you work eagerly and cheerfully? Does this area of your coaching need adjusting?

Scripture: Isaiah 40:11; John 10:11-15; 1 Corinthians 9:24-27

Prayer: *Lord, may our focus, our top priority, for our athletes be based on the things above, the eternal purpose: Your glory! In Christ's name, amen.*

Dreams

Now to Him who is able to do above and beyond all that we ask or think—according to the power that works in you—to Him be glory in the church and in Christ Jesus to all generations, forever and ever.

EPHESIANS 3:20-21

Every year I look at my team's schedule of games during preseason and start to calculate wins and losses. One game I'm certain we'll win; another we probably won't; still another will be a toss-up. Though each season is filled with uncertainty and challenges, most coaches I know still dream about championships and MVP awards. What's exciting to me is that God can do immeasurably more than all of these expectations combined.

In the apostle Paul's letter to his friends in Ephesus, he reminds them that God's ability far surpasses their dreams. According to the power that He works in those who believe, God is willing to go above and beyond what humans can imagine. In other words, God's reality is even bigger than anything we could dream!

This means that God's plans for each of us are even greater than any we could dream of on our own, and He proves that to us in the person of Jesus Christ. Who could have imagined that a perfect God would provide a way for imperfect people like us to come into His presence? But He did just that when Jesus took the penalty for our sins on the cross, becoming the bridge to a daily relationship with the Almighty! And because of His faithful provision of grace, we can absolutely trust God to make provision for our lives in ways that we can't even conceive. He is able to do immeasurably more than all we even know to ask or imagine. That's how great God's power is in our lives. His reality is bigger than our dreams!

Whatever challenges we as coaches face today, we can face them with the confidence that comes from God when we step into the reality of His plans, knowing that His life and power eclipse our wildest dreams! —*Roger Lipe*

1. What are your dreams for your team, your family and your personal life?

2. Is your influence for Christ limited by the size of your dreams?

3. What are your God-sized dreams?

Scripture: 1 Kings 3:7-14; John 14:12-14; Ephesians 3:14-20

Prayer: *Lord, thank You that Your dreams for me are greater than any I could imagine on my own. In Jesus Christ, amen.*

God is willing to go above and beyond what we can imagine. His reality is bigger than anything we could dream!

The Calling

He who calls you is faithful,
who also will do it.

1 THESSALONIANS 5:24

Many times on the Christian journey, we sense God calling us to do something. Sometimes, though, the task seems too great or our resources seem too small. Other times, God's call can feel overwhelming and cause us to doubt whether we really heard Him at all. Thankfully, He has given us His Scriptures to speak directly to our fears and doubts when it comes to matters related to His call.

The apostle Paul knew that his friends in Thessalonica sometimes struggled with whether they had heard God's call. So he wrote to them about why they could trust God when He asked them to do something, reminding them that God had never stopped being faithful to provide for them, lead them or be with them. In fact, in 1 Thessalonians 5:10, Paul wrote, "[Our Lord Jesus Christ] died for us so that, whether we are awake or asleep, we may live together with him" (*NIV*). God proved His faithfulness in the person of Jesus Christ, who took human doubts and fears to the cross!

Paul's words in 1 Thessalonians 5:24 is a marvelous promise for those who hear God's call to coach. It says nothing about the abilities of the hearer, but it speaks volumes about the One who does the calling. He is called faithful, that is, fully reliable to do that which He promised. Is there any greater encouragement? But He does not stop there: He says that He will bring it to pass. (That's much better than saying that He'd watch as we try to bring it to pass!)

This powerful verse causes me to trust in the Lord through this marvelous process called pursuing His will. He both calls us and carries out His will in us. Our part is to answer, to make ourselves available for His service and to look to Jesus who is proof of His faithfulness! —*Roger Lipe*

1. What does it mean to be called by God?

2. Do you see coaching as a job or a calling?

3. How do you know that you really heard God's call?

Scripture: Exodus 3:1-10; 1 Samuel 3:1-9; Luke 1:26-29

Prayer: *Gracious God, please give me ears to hear Your voice calling me to Yourself, and the confidence to respond for the sake of Your glory. Amen.*

No Knick Knocking!

Keep asking, and it will be given to you.
Keep searching, and you will find. Keep knocking,
and the door will be opened to you.
MATTHEW 7:7

Of all the silly games that I learned as a child, the one I remember best was a game some of the older kids in the neighborhood played—one that we didn't exactly brag about to our parents. "Knick Knocking" was the practice of approaching a neighbor's front door, knocking loudly several times, and then running away. Serious Knick Knockers would retreat to a nearby hideaway so that they could watch the unsuspecting neighbor open the door and search for a visitor. This was actually entertaining to the mischievous kids on our block!

The more I've grown in my Christian faith, the more I've come to realize how many of us play Knick Knocking when it comes to prayer. We bring a request before God and "knock" loudly, only to drop the prayer and run away before the door opens or an answer comes. But Jesus tells us to "keep knocking." He invites us to come right up to His doorstep, throw our knuckles across the door and make noise. Knocking requires effort, fast or slow, light or vigorous, but the key to knocking is repetition. We're supposed to keep at it until the door opens.

P. T. Forsyth wrote, "The chief failure of prayer is its cessation."[2] Sometimes we simply stop praying too soon. But the truth of the gospel says that because Jesus Christ made a way for us on the cross, we can come to our Father's house at any hour of the day or night and call on Him! He loves it when we come to Him! He never slumbers or sleeps (see Psalm 121:4), so we should never give up knocking or run away and wonder if He'll answer. He will! —*Kathy Malone*

1. Have you felt like you've kept "knocking" in prayer but no door has opened?

2. How do you deal with prayers that seem to go unanswered?

3. What do you think it means to "make noise" in prayer?

Scripture: Psalm 121:1-8; Luke 11:5-8; James 5:13-18

Prayer: *Dear God, stir up in me a desire to come to You again and again. Teach me to pray and not give up even when the answer seems far off. Increase my faith, Lord! Amen.*

> "Prayer is never rejected so long as we do not cease to pray. The chief failure of prayer is its cessation. Our importunity is a part of God's answer, both of His answer to us and ours to Him."
> —P. T. Forsyth

Measuring the Heart

> But the Lord said to Samuel, "Do not look at his appearance or his stature, because I have rejected him. Man does not see what the Lord sees, for man sees what is visible, but the Lord sees the heart."
>
> 1 SAMUEL 16:7

Another signing day has passed. The rankings are out, the top programs have locked down the "best" athletes in the country, and the "blue chippers," All-Americans and All-Stars have made their decisions. All of the gifts and abilities of these athletes, however, do not guarantee success. If teams are going to be successful, they must also have "heart." Yet, even in our culture of technological advances, no system exists that measures an athlete's heart.

God values our heart above our outward appearance or abilities. In the Old Testament story found in 1 Samuel 16:1-13, although Saul had great physical presence, he lost favor with God and was rejected as king. So, the prophet Samuel went to Bethlehem to the home of Jesse where he was to anoint one of Jesse's eight sons as the next king. Jesse lined them up before Samuel, sure that Eliab, his eldest, would be chosen. While Eliab's appearance was impressive, he was not God's choice. David, the youngest, was out tending sheep; his father hadn't even considered him for the job! But God knew David's heart was for Him, just as He knew His bigger plan for all humankind: that from the line of King David, another King would come—Jesus.

Over the next four years, many talented athletes—like Saul—will fade, and recruits with less glamour but more heart—like David—will surface. These athletes with heart will do whatever it takes to improve individually and as team members. They remind us that God is the Master Recruiter. If we were to stand before Him like Jesse's sons, would He choose us because of what He sees in our hearts? Would He see a heart that crowns Jesus as King? —*Charles Gee*

1. From a biblical viewpoint, what does it mean to have heart?
2. What players have you known who had average physical skills but great heart?
3. What qualities do these athletes with heart bring to the team?

Scripture: Deuteronomy 8:1-2; 1 Samuel 16:1-13; Luke 6:43-45

Prayer: *Lord, thank You for being more concerned with my heart than with the outward appearance of my life or career. Help me to crown Jesus as King in all I do and say, for His sake, amen.*

No Fear

There is no fear in love; but perfect love casts out fear.
1 JOHN 4:18, *NKJV*

I was in graduate school when the dean from a Christian college where I was working asked me to coach the women's field hockey team (the team's head coach had fallen ill). Although I loved playing field hockey, I had never considered coaching. But the players were due to arrive in two days, the dean looked desperate, and I didn't have the heart to say no. I knew the game like a close friend—how hard could it be?

Staring at the 25 women on that hot August morning—and with a week of training and a season of games ahead—I realized that I didn't have a clue as to what I was doing! Fear gripped me. I faked my way through the first day and stayed up all night prepping for the next week. Finally I prayed for *help*, telling God that I needed an *experienced* assistant.

Two weeks later, the dean found my assistant. On the day of practice, he walked toward the field with a guitar slung over his shoulder and a smile on his face. He said he knew nothing about field hockey but that he was ready to help!

My minstrel/assistant coach decided to begin each practice and game with a team song he wrote called "No Fear," which was based on 1 John 4:18 and 2 Timothy 1:7. *Ironic choice*, I thought. Every day, I stood on that field, sang those verses and remembered to love, not fear—to claim God's spirit of power and not be timid.

God did not send what I thought I needed that season, but He gave me what got me through: His promises in Jesus Christ. To think He even had the good humor to set it all to music on a hockey field! —*Eileen F. Sommi*

1. When you've cried to God for help, what (or whom) did He send?

2. How would having a spirit of power, love and discipline affect your coaching today?

3. How can you love your team and help them to have a spirit of love instead of timidity?

Scripture: Psalm 121:1-2; Isaiah 41:10-14; Matthew 14:30-31; Hebrews 4:15-16

Prayer: *Lord Jesus, fill me with Your spirit of love, power and discipline. Take my fear and send Your perfect help! Amen.*

> Therefore I remind you to stir up the gift of God which is in you through the laying on of my hands. For God has not given us a spirit of fear, but of power and of love and of a sound mind.
>
> 2 Timothy 1:6-7, NKJV

And let us be concerned about
one another in order to promote
love and good works.

HEBREWS 10:24

Coach Peacock's team had just won a state championship. They were celebrating in the locker room, and Coach was hugging his players right and left. As the congratulations continued, the coach noticed one player in particular sitting alone on a bench, watching him. Coach Peacock knew that the young man's parents were divorced and also that his dad was an alcoholic who never attended any of his son's games. So he walked over to the player and asked if he was okay. The young man responded, "Yes, Coach, but I was just wondering . . . could I have another hug?"

The experience was a milestone in Coach Peacock's life, so much so that he began a campaign to be a "team of huggers." He started with the coaching staff. Some on the staff were resistant to giving "real" hugs, but Coach Peacock wouldn't let them get away with a wimpy hug. It had to be a full-blown "bear hug." Soon, the coaches began sharing hugs with their players, and Coach Peacock found that hugs were a tremendously effective form of encouragement.

Most of us would agree that hugs encourage us and remind us that someone cares about us. Of course, there are many ways to encourage others. Hebrews 10:24 says that we are to consider how to stimulate and encourage one another to good deeds. Why? Because Jesus, the Son of God, willingly took on all of our discouragement on the cross so that we might experience the embrace of God's love. Because of that truth, let's consider all the ways that we might encourage our fellow coaches, teachers, players, family members and neighbors. —*Bill Burnett*

1. In what ways have other people encouraged you?

2. How have other coaches encouraged you?

3. What are some specific ways that you could encourage your players? Other coaches?

Scripture: Acts 15:30-32; Romans 15:4-6; Hebrews 3:12-13

Prayer: *God, how great that You would invite me to experience the embrace of Your love! May Your love always lead me as I consider how to encourage others. For Your glory, amen.*

Confidence Building

Therefore encourage one another and build each other up as you are already doing.
1 THESSALONIANS 5:11

Each contest that we're involved in as coaches is filled with missed opportunities, errors and mistakes. In some games, such as volleyball, basketball, softball and baseball, we have only a few seconds to respond to shortcomings or errors. In other sports, such as football, golf, and track and field, response time may be longer.

Regardless of the seconds or minutes that tick away, our reactions to our players' mistakes are critical, not only for their confidence but often for the outcome of the game.

That's why responding to an athlete's failures can be one of our greatest challenges. Whether in a crucial moment in the game or off the court or field, how we respond can empower or tear down an athlete. Throughout practices, games and other interactions with student-athletes, our goal should be to plant seeds of success that clearly demonstrate our belief in them. Our choice of words, the timing of those words and the manner in which we convey them has a powerful impact on their lives.

So if we are clear in our communication, constructive in our comments and direct in our feedback, expressing both personal compassion and a passion for excellence in the process, we can help take our athletes to a higher level.

As we help them look forward to the next opportunity instead of dwelling on their shortcomings, we'll reflect to them a portion of the mercy that we have all received as Christians. God has demonstrated to us the ultimate response to mistakes, or sin, in the person of Jesus Christ, and He empowers us to do the same.

Though we sin and fall short of His expectations, His mercy and love offered through Jesus' death and resurrection provide a new opportunity for each day as well as for eternity! —*Joel Schuldheisz*

1. When it comes to responding to mistakes, what situations challenge you the most?

2. How did Christ confront and respond to His disciples' mistakes?

3. What are some strategies we can follow that will instill confidence in our athletes and empower them to excel?

Scripture: Mark 11-21; John 11:1-16; 21:15-19

Prayer: *Thank You, God, for the love and compassion You show me when I fall short of Your expectations. Help me to inspire those with whom I interact to be what You know they could be. Amen.*

You did not choose Me, but I chose you. I appointed you that you should go out and produce fruit, and that your fruit should remain, so that whatever you ask the Father in My name, He will give you.

JOHN 15:16

When I was a kid, our neighborhood basketball court—the kind with the chain nets—was the place where everybody went to play the best basketball. During the summers, top college and high school players packed the court.

One day, I was chosen by a college player to be on his team—something I really didn't want to do. To me, the opposing team looked a lot more capable of winning. As I stood beside the college player, wishing that I were on the other team, he turned to me and said, "You don't want to be on our team, do you? I *chose* you, but I can tell that you don't want to be on our team." I hadn't said a word to him about it, but my body language had betrayed my thoughts. When he asked me if I wanted to be on the other team, I said yes. He responded, "Okay, go over there. We'll take Tommy instead." I went, and our team lost.

That college player, just by looking at me, could tell that I didn't want to commit to his team. When God chooses us and invites us to follow Him, thank goodness He doesn't change His mind if one day we don't look like we're much of a Christian! He never says, "Okay, go over there. I'll find someone else instead." In fact, the Bible says that He will leave the flock of 99 to search the hills for the one lost sheep (see Luke 15:4).

Even when we don't make winning decisions, Jesus Christ, our Good Shepherd, remains faithful in His devotion to us. His grace then becomes so irresistible that we'll never want to wander away from Him! And if for some reason we get a little distracted, He stands waiting for our return to His side. —*Les Steckel*

1. Do you base your daily decisions on Christ's commitment to you?

2. How can His devotion *to* you inspire devotion *from* you?

3. What does it feel like to be chosen by God?

Scripture: Joshua 24:14-15; John 15:11-17; 1 Corinthians 15:58

Prayer: *Thank You, God, for seeking me and choosing me to be Your disciple! I ask that You would help me to bear fruit today that reflects Your devotion. Amen.*

First Response

Listen to my words, Lord; consider my sighing.
Pay attention to the sound of my cry, my King
and my God, for I pray to You. At daybreak,
Lord, You hear my voice; at daybreak I plead
my case to You and watch expectantly.

PSALM 5:1-3

When problems come into our lives, we all respond in various ways. A "thinker" chews on the problem and looks at it from every possible angle. A "talker" seeks the wisdom and advice of others. A "doer" goes at the problem head-on and works hard to find a solution. A "reactor" has a negative emotional outburst and explodes in the midst of difficulty.

But I believe that God wants our first response to be prayer, though that isn't often our first reaction. No matter how big or small our problems are, He wants us to present our requests to Him first. As Psalm 55:22 says, "Cast your burden on the Lord, and He will support you; He will never allow the righteous to be shaken."

The daily situations that cross my path as a coach are many: recruiting battles, disciplinary action, frustrations with a player's performance, conflict with a staff member, and so on. As a role model to my players and fellow coaches, I am convicted daily as to how I respond when problems arise. The Lord wants nothing more than for our first response to be to lay our requests at His feet and to open our hearts to hear His voice.

From our early years in grade school, we have been taught to dial 911 as our first response to an emergency. Perhaps our spiritual 911 should be to allow the love and presence of the Triune God to fill us and to wait patiently for His answer! —*Lisa Fisher*

1. How do you respond when a problem arises?

2. What areas in your coaching have you not directed to the Lord? Why?

3. By changing your first response, how can you see this affecting your coaching in a positive way?

Scripture: Matthew 11:28-29; Philippians 4:6; 2 Thessalonians 3:5

Prayer: *Lord, I pray that my first response today would be to come to You in challenging times. Thank You for wanting to bear my burden. I pray that by coming to You first, I will be an example to my players and fellow coaches of the peace, love and grace that come through Your Son, Jesus Christ. Amen.*

No matter how big or how small our problems are, God wants us to present our requests to Him first.

**Now there are different gifts,
but the same Spirit.**
1 CORINTHIANS 12:4

The Boston Red Sox saw little potential in their 24-year-old pitcher. He'd had a couple of decent years, but he had showed little sign of improvement. Eventually, the team traded him to the New York Yankees, who decided to move him to the outfield to utilize his strong arm. The Yankees also believed that he could become a good hitter. They were right. Years later, few people remember that Babe Ruth began his career as a mediocre pitcher in Boston!

Different athletes are blessed with different skills and physical traits, and each makes them more effective in some positions than in others. A football player who is 5' 10" and 200 pounds might be a tremendous running back, but he would struggle as a wide receiver. A 7' 2" basketball player would likely be unsuccessful playing point guard. It is vitally important for a coach to find the position that allows the athlete to use his or her skills to the fullest. Athletes in the wrong position may still perform adequately, but they will never reach their full potential.

Christians must also find the right position. Paul teaches us in 1 Corinthians 12 that different Christians are given different gifts. For example, some are gifted teachers, while others are gifted administrators. There are few joys in life as great as using our gifts in God's service. Conversely, there are few frustrations as great as attempting to serve in an area in which we aren't gifted. But when the right talent is matched with the right job, great things happen. As Christians, we should never feel compelled to work in an area in which we are not gifted. Rather, we should wait on the Lord and His counsel. God will give us the opportunity and grace through Jesus Christ to use the gifts He has given us. We all need to identify our gifts and find the right place to use them! —*Michael Wiggins*

1. What are some things that you do that give you a sense of accomplishment or satisfaction?

2. When have you most felt God's pleasure?

3. What gifts or talents has God provided you with and how do you use them?

Scripture: Exodus 35:10; Romans 12:3-8; 1 Corinthians 12; 1 Timothy 4:14-16

Prayer: *Thank You, Lord, that each member in the Body of Christ is gifted and equally important. Enable me today to use my gifts to serve Your Body!*

Smack

Jesus answered, "I am the way and the truth and the life. No one comes to the Father except through me."

JOHN 14:6, *NIV*

We hear it on ESPN, read it in the papers and see it on the nightly news. What is it? "Smack" is the vernacular talk that some players and coaches use to dramatize or publicize their performances. It is hyper-bragging mixed with trash talking! Unfortunately, in every league, game and team, it's easy to find someone who's gifted at talking smack. Usually, the person who talks this way has an ego the size of Texas but humility and common sense the size of an M&M. Smack talkers can talk the talk, but they rarely walk the walk.

Back in Jerusalem, there was a group of men who could talk spiritual smack with the best of them. We know them as the Pharisees—and Caiaphas was their top dog. The irony, of course, was that

Caiaphas and his buddies thought Jesus and His followers were the trash talkers. But Jesus only spoke the truth.

No verse better illustrates this than John 14:6, where Jesus said that the only way to His heavenly Father is through Him. Many self-righteous men thought such a claim was the ultimate smack; some called it blasphemy. After all, no sane man ever talked like this, so it's not hard to understand why the Pharisees thought Jesus could not back up His words! But they soon watched Him both talk the talk and walk the walk. What He said was true because Jesus *is* the Truth, the Way and the Life. The only way to the holy Father is through the sacrificial death of His holy Son!

So when we acknowledge Jesus as the Way, the Truth and the Life and that His work on the cross did all the talking for us, our daily lives will reflect His. That's the one sure way that our walk can match our spiritual talk! —*Jere Johnson*

1. Athletically or spiritually speaking, are you a smack talker?

2. Does your walk match your talk?

3. How can you be more like Christ?

Scripture: John 11:24-27; Ephesians 4:17-32; 1 Timothy 4:6-9

Prayer: *Gracious God, You alone have provided all we need in the person of Jesus, Your Son, who lived, died and rose again that we might be Your words and deeds to a world in need of both! Amen.*

> **Smack** \smak\ *n*: Vernacular talk used by some players and coaches to dramatize or publicize their performances.

Exit the Roller Coaster

About midnight Paul and Silas were praying
and singing hymns to God, and the [other]
prisoners were listening to them.
ACTS 16:25

Whoever said life is a roller coaster must have been a coach. It seems that on a daily basis, the coaching profession can send us rocketing toward glorious, adrenaline-boosted highs. But it can also throw us into a downward spiral with exasperating emotional lows.

One of our best opportunities to be witnesses to our players is to show them that, as Christians, our emotions aren't bound to these ups and downs. If we appear to be exuberant when we are winning but seem nearly suicidal after a bad practice, we are not modeling the consistent joy of Christ. Our players need to see that our joy is not based on what they do or do not do, but that it is based entirely on what Christ did for us at Calvary. The reality of His death and resurrection is the source of our daily and eternal joy! That means we can honor God on good *and* bad days. As author Jerry Bridges wrote, "The purpose of joy is to glorify God by demonstrating to an unbelieving world that our loving and faithful heavenly Father cares for us and provides for us all that we need."[3]

So let's exit the emotional roller coaster. Let's remember that Paul and Silas remained joyful throughout their imprisonment and sang praises to God in their jail cells *because* they knew in whom they had placed their faith! Surely, we too can remain joyful in Jesus throughout our seasons and give God the glory He deserves in our locker rooms! —*Chanda Husser Rigby*

1. Does your team feel like your happiness is based on its performance?

2. How can you exemplify that joy in Christ does not depend on any earthly circumstances?

3. Where does your joy come from?

Scripture: Psalms 43:1-5; 51:10-13; Philippians 4:11-13

Prayer: *Eternal God, please fill me with Your everlasting joy so that my life might be a reflection of Your constant love. In Jesus' name, amen.*

BIG GOD, Little Me

Neither is He served by human hands, as though He needed anything, since He Himself gives everyone life and breath and all things.

ACTS 17:25

Coaches are familiar with famous slogans. We put them on T-shirts, in pictures or paint them on walls to try to motivate our athletes. One famous slogan is, "TEAM, me." "Team" is capitalized because that's where everyone's focus should be. "Me" is in lower case to show that the individual's goals are secondary to the team's goals.

A great slogan for the Christian life could be, "GOD, me." It's easy to understand the concept of a big God because we all know that He is bigger than we are. The hard part is allowing Him to reign over all that we do. Because most coaches are competitors and problem solvers, we feel the need to do everything that we can for our programs. We put so much pressure on ourselves to have a great program that we sometimes lose perspective and forget to have fun.

As Christians we often do the same thing. We put pressure on ourselves to live a perfect life and do all these Christian "things" because we think that's what it's about. We get so busy and tired that we lose the joy of knowing Jesus.

But God wants our relationship with Him to be a joy, not a burden. Acts 17:25 says that He will give us everything we really need (not necessarily everything we want!). In fact, He already has in the person and sacrifice of Jesus Christ! Why, then, do many of us feel that we have to perform all these spiritual deeds when all God wants for us is to believe and trust Him each day?

If we'll focus more on knowing Him and less on doing, we'll experience the presence of God Almighty as He walks beside us in all that we do! Our hearts will be redirected to our real source of joy and our lives—not a slogan—will reflect that to others! —*Scott Jackson*

1. What are things that you feel you "need" to do for Christ?

2. How can the joy of Jesus affect your coaching?

3. What prevents you from relaxing in God's presence?

Scripture: Matthew 11:25-30; Luke 10:38-41; Acts 17:22-29

Prayer: *Lord, quiet my heart and mind from the busyness of life so that I can hear Your voice today and sense Your presence. Amen.*

It's easy to understand the concept of a big God—the hard part is allowing Him to reign over all we do.

> Before God and Christ Jesus, who is going to
> judge the living and the dead, and by His appearing
> and His kingdom, I solemnly charge you: proclaim
> the message; persist in it whether convenient
> or not; rebuke, correct, and encourage with
> great patience and teaching.
>
> 2 TIMOTHY 4:1-2

One day, I was leaving my office late after a challenging afternoon. Just as I was locking the door, a student whom I barely knew asked if I were on my way home. My initial thought was that since I'd already worked later than usual and I was tired, I'd ask him to come back tomorrow. But I noticed something in his eyes, so I unlocked my door and invited him in.

Then he stunned me with his question: He wanted to know why I was always kind to him and other athletes! Considering how only seconds earlier I was about to tell him to come back later, I realized that I was being given an opportunity to tell a young man what motivated me to care about him. As a result of staying a few minutes late, I was able to share with him the good news of Jesus Christ, who cared so much for us that He took the punishment for our sins on Himself by going to the cross.

The opportunities that the Lord places in front of us might not always seem convenient, but they always have eternal significance. If we are to influence the people around us (particularly the athletes we coach), we must be ready—even when we'd rather do something else—to represent Christ by our words, thoughts and actions. We must yield to the person and work of Jesus living in us so that the people He sends our way are loved with His love. We never know how He might lead us! —*Ken Kladnik*

1. What are some opportunities that you have missed because of busyness?

2. Think about when you have made time for another person. What was the outcome?

3. How can your door be more open to others?

Scripture: Luke 10:38-42; Galatians 5:16-26; Ephesians 5:1-2,15-16

Prayer: *Lord, use me today to share the good news of Your kingdom. Help me to not allow the world's distractions to keep me from doing Your will. Thank You for each opportunity that will present itself as You lead me by Your Holy Spirit. Amen.*

The Eternal Purpose

For the Son of Man has come to seek and to save the lost.
LUKE 19:10

Athletes must know their purpose on the team. For instance, an offensive lineman's purpose is to protect the quarterback and create space for the running back. A pitcher's purpose is not to allow a batter to get a hit. A goalkeeper's purpose on the soccer field is to keep the ball from getting into the net. For a team to succeed, each player must use his or her talent and experience to help the team accomplish the overall purpose: victory. If we do not have the players with the right skills or fail to place a player in the proper position, the team will have difficulty attaining its goals.

Just as athletes need to know their purpose, each coach has a specific purpose as well. An assistant coach may be in charge of one aspect of the team, such as being the offensive coordinator or leading the team in pre-practice stretches. Head coaches have another purpose: to mold and shape the lives of young people.

Jesus had a purpose, too. His was single-minded and simple: to seek and to save the lost. This was the reason behind His entire life on Earth and why He chose to die on the cross: to bring us to Himself! He knows His players' gifts and talents, and He knows exactly where we should be placed. As members of Team Jesus Christ, we must serve our Team Captain by doing His Father's will. Jesus came to Earth as man in order that we might be with Him for all eternity! Today, as we understand our purpose on His team, let's serve Him by spreading His message to all who will listen! —*Michael Hill*

1. What purpose has God given you in your current role?

2. How are you serving Jesus in that role?

3. What might keep you from really believing that Christ's work on the cross was to save *you*?

Scripture: John 10:9; Romans 5:8; Ephesians 2:8-9; 1 John 5:9-10

Prayer: *Father, help me today to seek Your will for my life. Thank You for uniquely creating me to help accomplish Your purposes for others! Amen.*

I am the way, the truth, and the life. No one comes to the Father except through Me. If you know Me, you will also know My Father. From now on you do know Him and have seen Him.

John 14:6-7

> From now on, then, we do not know anyone in a
> purely human way. Even if we have known Christ in
> a purely human way, yet now we no longer know Him
> like that. Therefore if anyone is in Christ, there is
> a new creation; old things have passed away,
> and look, new things have come.
>
> 2 CORINTHIANS 5:16-17

In our pregame talks, we tell our players to "play with heart!" and encourage them to perform their best. The more our players develop such a vision, the deeper their commitment to the sport becomes. This is exactly what Jesus wants from us. He wants to develop a heart in us that will commit to knowing Him in a deeper, more intimate way. As David said in Psalm 51:10, "God, create a clean heart for me and renew a steadfast spirit within me." As we develop this kind of heart, others will notice.

For years, I believed in who God was, but I did not have a relationship with Him. The only relationship I thought that I could count on was my relationship with my grandparents. Then the Lord brought a friend into my life to "coach" me into wanting a relationship with Him. She cared enough about me to show me her heart. As a result, I was so drawn to Jesus that I surrendered and made Him more than my Savior—He became the Lord of my life. As I learned to trust Him and accept His grace and compassion, all of my relationships changed. So did my coaching!

As coaches who follow Christ, we can pour out to others what He has poured into us. He'll restore and rejuvenate our relationships as He continues to change our hearts. And as we rest in Him and continue to be transformed into His likeness, the peace, hope and joy we experience with Him will show our players what it really means to play with heart! —*Lisa Phillips*

1. How would you describe your team's heart? Your heart?

2. Think of those people whom God put in your life to model heart and faith. How could you now encourage them?

3. In what ways has your life become new since acknowledging Jesus as Lord?

Scripture: Psalm 51; Matthew 22:37-40; Ephesians 3:19

Prayer: *Lord, I pray as David prayed that You would create in me a clean heart for Your purposes. Amen.*

Self-Sacrifice

Peter began to tell Him, "Look, we have left everything and followed You."
MARK 10:28

When most sport seasons end, numbers get crunched. As coaches, it's easy for us to get caught up in this number crunching, especially as the media highlights our career wins, the titles we've won and the number of "Coach of the Year" awards we've received.

But any true coach knows that records are not what are important. Having the opportunity to work with athletes and make a difference in their lives is what is important. Coaches, like players, make a lot of sacrifices to develop winning teams, but most will tell you those sacrifices and successes are for the athletes—for the joy of watching players mature and grow.

In the Christian life, we make sacrifices as well. Instead of sitting in front of the television after a long day, we volunteer for church committees, sing in the choir, or work in the soup kitchen. What motivates us to do these things? If it is to build up a store of good deeds, then we're more concerned with building a record as Christians than with honoring Christ. In other words, our "sacrificial" serving isn't really serving anyone but ourselves.

In his book *My Utmost for His Highest*, Oswald Chambers asks:

> Have you ever been driven to do something for God not because you felt that it was useful or your duty to do so, or that there was anything in it for you, *but simply because you love Him?*[4]

As a Christian, I am called to serve Christ because I love Him, not because I need to earn His love. In fact, there is nothing that I could do to earn His love—Christ already paid the price for that love when He died on the cross!

We are not called to serve Christ for personal gain, for like Peter, we have left everything to follow Jesus! For Christian coaches, genuine love for our athletes motivates a selfless commitment to them. Winning takes care of itself. —*Donna Miller*

1. Are you more concerned about your players' successes, as individuals and as athletes, than you are about your own coaching accomplishments?

2. What motivates your "good deeds"?

3. What steps can you take to keep your motives on track—both as a coach and as a child of God?

Scripture: Acts 20:24; Galatians 2:19-20; Philippians 3:7-11

Prayer: *Please remind me, oh God, that nothing compares to knowing Christ Jesus my Lord! Amen.*

Think Before You Speak

The one who guards his mouth protects his life; the one who opens his lips invites his own ruin.

PROVERBS 13:3

As a young coach I had a short fuse, especially when it came to dealing with men in stripes. It was hard keeping my mouth shut, and I often said things that got me in trouble. One game in particular, I thought my team was being treated unfairly, and I was quick to point it out. Late in the game, I stood up and yelled, "What?!" It was only one word, but the officials had heard enough. I got a technical foul that cost my team the game.

Controlling the tongue is a problem for many coaches and athletes. Many times, we create more problems with our mouths than with our actions. Why? In my case, it was because I wouldn't think before I spoke. Proverbs 13:3 tells us that if we can control our tongues, it will enhance our lives. But if we speak before we think, we can ruin everything.

Why does God want us to keep our tongues in check? When we speak before thinking, we usually do not honor Him with our speech. He would much rather we say nothing at all than speak too quickly. One of the best illustrations of this is when Christ was brought before Pontius Pilate and did not open His mouth to defend Himself against false accusations. He knew that God could have sent a thousand angels to defend Him, but He trusted the One who ordered the heavens and earth. The prophet Isaiah described Jesus this way: "He was oppressed and afflicted, yet He did not open His mouth. Like a lamb led to the slaughter and like a sheep silent before her shearers, He did not open His mouth" (Isaiah 53:7).

It's the most difficult thing in the world to tame the tongue, but God's Spirit living in us through the work of Jesus can help us think before we speak—even in the most challenging situations! —*Jere Johnson*

1. How can you speak life to those around you?

2. When was the last time your tongue got you in trouble?

3. What can you do to start thinking before you speak?

Scripture: Matthew 5:36-37; Ephesians 4:29; James 1:19-20; 1 Peter 4:11

Prayer: *Living Word, please fill me with Your Spirit so that every word that comes out of my mouth today honors You! Amen.*

Following the Rules

Carefully follow [them], for this will [show] your wisdom and understanding in the eyes of the peoples. When they hear about all these statutes, they will say, "This great nation is indeed a wise and understanding people." For what great nation is there that has a god near to it as the Lord our God is [to us] whenever we call to Him?

DEUTERONOMY 4:6-7

Each new season starts out with a team meeting in which the coach goes over the team rules and gives the expectations for the upcoming season. During this time, the coach makes sure that there is no question as to what will be required from the athletes.

The head coach will expect the players to follow the team rules, and he or she will generally set out rewards to the team for doing so. These rewards might include a letterman's patch or pin, or they might include a lessened conditioning in practice. Whatever these happen to be, the head coach makes sure that the team knows the rewards for following the team rules.

God is the Ultimate Head Coach. Just as a good earthly head coach goes over the rules, so does our Ultimate Head Coach. God gave His "team rules" to the Israelites through Moses, and He expected His team to follow those rules.

Like our coaches here on Earth, the Ultimate Head Coach also has different rewards for following His rules. But these rewards are not only earthly, but they are also eternal. And knowing that you've impacted the kingdom of God is better than a letterman's jacket any day. —*Michael Hill*

1. Do you know the team rules?

2. Are you following the team rules?

3. What rules do you have difficulty following?

Scripture: Matthew 5:33-38; 16:27; Luke 6:35; Colossians 3:23-24

Prayer: *Lord, show me Your ways. Give me an understanding of Your team rules so that I might be a light in the dark world. Amen.*

The Fellowship of Christian Athletes Values
Integrity: Attend carefully to your private and public walk with God.

Serving: Seek to serve your athletes as Christ served the Church.

Teamwork: Do not boast in your abilities or believe in your own strength.

Excellence: Be a competitor by conviction and a disciple of determination.

Don't gloat when your enemy falls, and don't let your heart rejoice when he stumbles, or the Lord will see, be displeased, and turn His wrath away from him.

PROVERBS 24:17-18

In 2001, golfer Annika Sorenstam dominated the women's professional tour, winning eight tournaments and topping two million dollars in earnings. After that phenomenal year, Annika's chief rival, Karrie Webb, commented that she'd eat her hat if Annika won eight tournaments in the coming year. The following season, Annika won eleven tournaments and earned nearly three million dollars in prize money.

Sometimes the competition is too strong. The fact remains, though, we can't win them all. John Wooden didn't win every basketball game that he coached. Jack Nicklaus didn't win every golf tournament that he entered. Cy Young didn't win every baseball game that he pitched. Mature coaches and athletes take it a step further; they learn to appreciate the competition's performance. No athlete enjoys losing or is content with losing. When the inevitable loss occurs, however, the true sportsman or woman appreciates the performance of the victor and congratulates the opponent on a job well done.

We all know that even Christians can sometimes struggle to celebrate the victories of others. Perhaps someone else got the job or a cross-town rival won the tournament. Whatever the situation, we have a tendency to focus more on our loss than on the other person's gain. But the mature Christian recognizes God's will in every aspect of life, knowing that His perfect will may involve losses or apparent setbacks. After all, the suffering and death of Jesus Christ was God's plan!

How we respond to these situations reveals what is in our hearts. While the world expects bitterness and resentment in defeat, Christians can stand out by congratulating the victor, knowing that Christ has already won the ultimate victory for us. Not only will this simple act gain the respect of others, it will also make us more gracious on those occasions when we're the victors. —*Michael Wiggins*

1. How do you react to another coach's success?

2. What are some of the greatest lessons you've learned from your losses?

3. How do you teach your players to respond to victories and to defeats?

Scripture: Jonah 3:1-4:3; Luke 15:11-32; 1 John 2:3-11

Prayer: *Lord, empower me to live today with the grace and integrity of Your will! Amen.*

Troubled?

Your heart must not be troubled.
Believe in God; believe also in Me.
JOHN 14:1

Trouble and being troubled are two completely different things. Trouble is being down by a run, nobody on base, with two outs in the bottom of the ninth and our worst hitter coming to the plate. Being troubled is having no strategy for this scenario and not being prepared to accept the possible consequences that are about to come.

As coaches, there will be many times when we will have to declare to our team, "Don't worry, everything will be okay." We might even complete our short speech with the same words that Jesus did: "Believe in me." But if we haven't demonstrated believability to our players, these words will have absolutely no value. Without having the same credibility that Jesus had, our words will be like wisps of air.

In John 14:1, Jesus told His disciples, "Your heart must not be troubled. Believe in God; believe also in Me." Through His words,

Christ offered His followers comfort for the difficult days ahead. He knew that they were about to face some major trouble—serious persecution and, for some, even death. Jesus knew that trouble was coming for Him and for His followers, but He didn't want them to be troubled while facing it. And He doesn't want us to be troubled either.

As coaches, we need to aim high in becoming trustworthy to help our student athletes reach their potential. If our players can't trust us, then why should they follow us? Of course, God is the only one worthy of total trust—confirmed through Christ's willing sacrifice on the cross—but His new life inside us can make us trustworthy as well.

He invites us in the midst of any trouble that we are experiencing to bring our troubled hearts to our trustworthy God. Because even when our hearts are troubled, the ultimate remedy is still the same—totally trusting the Lord! —*Clay Elliot*

1. How have you faced a troubled situation?

2. Are your words like wisps of air to your team, or are they credible and valued?

3. What in the past has helped you face trouble?

Scripture: 2 Samuel 24:10; Luke 24:36-49; John 14:27-31

Prayer: *Lord, if trouble comes today, help me to come to You, believing that You will work it out according to Your good purposes! Thank You in Christ's name, amen.*

> Without having the same credibility that Jesus had, our words to our players will be like wisps of air.

And don't give the Devil an opportunity.
EPHESIANS 4:27

In the 1980s, the San Francisco 49ers made popular what became known as the West Coast Offense, an offense characterized by short, controlled-pass plays that gained only five to six yards. By running such low-risk plays, San Francisco nibbled away at their opponents. Even strong defensive opponents who never gave up "big plays" were humbled by the 49ers' consistent gains. San Francisco's strategy earned them five Super Bowl titles between 1982 and 1995.

Sports highlight shows are filled with replays of big plays: the breakaway goal, the 60-yard touchdown pass or the long homerun. Although these are exciting, rarely is a sporting event won in a single play. Certainly, the big play may put the nail in the coffin of an opponent, but often there are several small plays that lead to the loser's demise. The key to winning often involves staying close to the opposing team, nibbling away at them until success is reached. This allows the team to capitalize on the mistakes of their opponents and benefit from the opportunities that they are given.

Christians must be aware that our opponent uses a similar strategy. If we allow Satan to "stay close," he'll find a way to break down our defense. He doesn't need the big play to be successful, only enough small plays to capitalize on our mistakes. To overcome this strategy, we have to put him away early in the game, remembering that Jesus has already won the victory. Christ's sacrificial love for us invites us to turn every area of our lives over to Him. This means giving up those pet sins that allow Satan to nibble away at us. Every questionable move, every little lie, every fit of anger keeps our opponent in the game. But by turning away from these through confession and by focusing our lives on the power of the cross of Jesus Christ, we leave the enemy in the dust! —*Michael Wiggins*

1. Are you allowing Satan to stay close? If so, how?

2. Are there people or things in your life that are nibbling away at you?

3. When those nibbles occur, how do you react?

Scripture: Genesis 3:14; Proverbs 1:10-19; James 1:13-16; 1 Peter 5:8-9

Prayer: *Lord, help me to stay close to You today and live in the freedom of Your grace! Amen.*

God's Grace

My soul, praise the Lord, and do not forget all His benefits. He forgives all your sin; He heals all your diseases. He redeems your life from the Pit; He crowns you with faithful love and compassion. He satisfies you with goodness; your youth is renewed like the eagle.

PSALM 103:2-5

If we were to count on our hands the number of times someone has let us down or the number of times we've disappointed someone else, we'd definitely run out of fingers! As humans, we fail all the time, whether it be in our relationships, careers or daily disciplines. In fact, our life on Earth seems full of opportunities to learn from our mistakes. So it's a good thing that we have promises like Psalm 103:12: "As far as the east is from the west, so far has He removed our transgressions from us."

But an incredible thing happens when we begin to see ourselves through the eyes of our heavenly Father. No matter what mistakes we make, no matter the pain or regret we might feel, in God's eyes we shine brightly. How is it possible that He would see us as righteous and dearly loved? As the old hymn "Before the Throne of God Above" puts it:

Because the sinless Savior died, my sinful soul is counted free! For God the Just is satisfied, to look on Him and pardon me.[5]

Because of the perfect life of Jesus Christ on Earth, we can move beyond those feelings of inadequacy and shame to partake of His transforming grace! His presence in our daily lives redeems us, rescues us from the pit and showers us with love and compassion. Yes, He satisfies our desires with wonderful things! And no matter where we've been or what we've done, God continually invites us to Himself so that He can restore us and use us for His purposes—especially when we see ourselves through His eyes of grace! —*Danny Burns*

1. What causes you to be ashamed of your actions?

2. Do you realize that you are loved and forgiven?

3. What can you do to become the bright creation God sees?

Scripture: Micah 7:18-19; Luke 15:1-7; Romans 5:1-11; 1 John 3:1-3

Prayer: *Lord God, change my heart today that I might be confident of Your love, and fill my mind with thoughts of Your grace so that others might also know You! In Christ's name, amen.*

God and the Apple

After Jesus was baptized, He went up immediately from the water. The heavens suddenly opened for Him, and He saw the Spirit of God descending like a dove and coming down on Him. And there came a voice from heaven: "This is My beloved Son. I take delight in Him!"

MATTHEW 3:16-17

While I was eating lunch one day in the teacher's lounge, I overheard an office aide talking with her friend. The office aide could not understand how God could be God and Jesus at the same time—how He could be in heaven and on Earth at the same time! Her friend didn't know how to respond.

I asked God to give me the words to help them understand this difficult concept, and the Lord, being gracious, brought an idea to my mind. So, feeling confident, I got up from my table and went to tell them about God and an apple.

I started by explaining how an apple has a core (from which the apple comes to be), an inside white part, and an outer peel that makes up the skin of the apple. I then explained that God the Father is like the core of the apple; all things are created from Him. God the Holy Spirit is like the white part of the apple; He comes to live inside us at the point of salvation and gives us guidance. God the Son, Jesus, is like the outside of the apple; He took on a human "peeling" to show us that He experienced the same sufferings and temptations that we do. Yet He remained blameless. So Jesus, in human peeling, took our blame and sin so that we could be blameless in the Father's sight.

As coaches, we often have teachable moments like these that allow us to help our players and colleagues understand Christian truths. Thankfully, the idea about the three parts of an apple was just what I needed that day to explain how God the Father, God the Holy Spirit, and God the Son are one! —*Laura Crawford*

1. Is God the Father the core of your life?

2. How can you allow God the Holy Spirit to move inside of you?

3. In what ways can God the Son's example direct you today?

Scripture: Matthew 7:17-20; Acts 1:4-8; 1 Corinthians 1:9

Prayer: *Lord, help me take in all that You are in order for me to be all that You want me to be! Amen.*

Know the Source

No wisdom, no understanding, and no counsel [will prevail] against the Lord. A horse is prepared for the day of battle, but victory comes from the Lord.

PROVERBS 21:30-31

In 1982, the Miami Dolphins football team faced the New England Patriots at Schaefer Stadium in Foxboro, Massachusetts. Snow began to fall during the game, and by the fourth quarter the wintry conditions had contributed to a scoreless tie.

But late in the game, the Patriots drove down the field and came within field-goal range, where a successful kick would likely win the game. The New England coach ordered a snowplow to clear a spot for the kicking team, enabling the kicker to set his foot firmly on the turf. As a result, he kicked the game-winning field goal.

Tremendous preparation goes into competing at high levels. Coaches put athletes through drills to condition their bodies and teach athletes strategies to prepare their minds. Still, many of the variables associated with winning are outside of the control of the coach. Weather conditions, travel situations and lucky bounces all play a part in achieving victory. Experienced coaches prepare for the factors that are within their control and accept those that are outside their control.

As Christians, we are faced with the reality of uncontrollable factors when we share our faith with others. We can say all the right words at all the right times, and yet we may never see someone make a decision for Christ. Thankfully, God does not check our win-loss record!

Some of the people that we encounter will accept with great joy the message that Jesus Christ loved them so much that He gave His life for them. Sadly, others will reject it, and sometimes we will never know the outcome. Even so, we must take every opportunity to testify to Christ by living out our faith with integrity, trusting that God's Spirit will work according to His purposes! —*Michael Wiggins*

1. What opportunities have you had to share your faith in word or by example?

2. How would you summarize the gospel message to someone who asked?

3. Who are some people in your life for whom you can pray to receive Jesus Christ?

Scripture: Matthew 13:1-23; 28:16-20; Luke 9:1-6; Acts 8:26-40

Prayer: *Almighty God, Your ways are perfect and Your love is unconditional. Help me to reflect that love to others today that they may know You! In Christ's name, amen.*

Talk Is Cheap

To the pure, everything is pure, but to those
who are defiled and unbelieving nothing is pure;
in fact, both their mind and conscience are defiled.
They profess to know God, but they deny Him by
their works. They are detestable, disobedient,
and disqualified for any good work.

TITUS 1:15-16

One of my favorite sayings as a coach was "Don't tell me. Show me." Today, however, some athletes have a hard time backing up what they say. They talk a good game, but they can't always live it out.

In the same way, the apostle Paul knew how easy it was for people to talk about Christ without having their lives match their words. That's why he encouraged true believers to stand strong; he did not want them to end up with empty lifestyles, like those he called, "detestable, disobedient, and disqualified for any good work." Like James, who encouraged Christians to "be doers of the word and not hearers only" (see James 1:22), Paul knew the importance of walking the talk. Christ had called him—like He calls each of us—to follow Him and love Him with his life and his words. God's standard is clear for us as well: He does not want us to be examples of cheap talk. Rather, He desires that our lives and our words reflect the Living Word, the One who gave up all so that we might be rich in good deeds!

We all want to believe that our players will do what they say they will. But we also know that isn't always the case. If we can inspire them to talk less and do more, we will be leading them into success *and* integrity. Jesus wants the same for His believers. He wants us to talk less about all the great things we intend to do for Him and start doing them. He wants us to imitate the same lifestyle of action that He exemplified, not one of mere talk. —*Jere Johnson*

1. Are you a talker or a doer?

2. How can you move beyond talk to loving actions?

3. In what ways can your deeds reflect Christ today?

Scripture: Titus 3:3-8; James 1:22-25; 1 John 3:18-20

Prayer: *Almighty Father, may my life and all I do speak of the Living Word, the hope of all humankind! Amen.*

God's Fearless Warrior

Then David said, "The Lord who rescued me from the paw of the lion and the paw of the bear will rescue me from the hand of this Philistine." Saul said to David, "Go, and may the Lord be with you."

1 SAMUEL 17:37

One of my favorite Bible stories is David versus Goliath. David was small, weaker than most his age and, by the world's standards, not prepared to play in the "big game" against the Philistines.

If we had read the pregame report for this battle, David would not have been on the roster. But David surprised everyone. He was empowered by his belief in a God who could overcome any obstacle or challenge—even a Philistine giant!

My "David" experience came after a game against our league rival. As expected, our team's invitation for postgame prayer had been met with rejection from the opposing team.

As our team gathered, however, I looked at our sea of white jerseys and saw one solitary blue jersey. In the middle of our huddle sat my "David"! His jersey was clean, he didn't weigh more than 150 pounds, and he looked more like a manager than a football player. But he had come to pray.

What happened next was amazing. Some of "David's" teammates from the opposing side noticed that he was with us. I don't know what motivated them, but one by one, his teammates joined our team for prayer. "David" had stepped out in faith to do what he knew his God wanted him to do, and that one step had an impact on hundreds of people that night!

As coaches, we are challenged every day to do what is right. As coaches committed to Jesus, the one who offered Himself for our sake, we are called to do what is right regardless of the obstacles or costs.

David could have lost his life by fighting Goliath. My "David" could have lost his reputation by praying with our team. With each individual, God was faithful and produced a great victory. —*Jim Shapiro*

1. How could David's example inspire you to step out for Jesus?

2. In what ways can you prepare your student-athletes for their "David" experience?

3. Are you facing any challenges or obstacles in which God needs to intervene?

Scripture: Numbers 14:1-10; 1 Samuel 17:20-37; Daniel 3:8-18

Prayer: *Thank You, Lord God of all, that You are mightier and more powerful than any challenge I am facing. Increase my faith in Your abilities! Amen.*

C'mon, Blue!

But the fruit of the Spirit is love, joy, peace, patience, kindness, goodness, faith, gentleness, self-control. Against such things there is no law.

GALATIANS 5:22-23

I love baseball! It is an individual sport that relies on a team for a successful outcome. It also is the only American sport in which, during a stoppage in play, a manager or coach can approach an umpire to dispute a rule or argue a call. Unfortunately, we've all seen a manager throwing a tantrum, kicking dirt on the plate or verbally abusing an umpire. And we've also seen the umpire retaliating in anger and, sometimes, losing control. It's hard to have someone yell at us or challenge our character in any setting, but especially in front of peers and spectators in a stadium.

In Galatians 5:22-23, the apostle Paul wrote that when the Holy Spirit dwells in us, He produces self-control in us. We can't obtain this fruit by natural means—it is produced only when we give Christ control over our lives. Granted, our sinful nature wants to yell, get angry, show off or get the last word. Even though I've been a Christian for 25 years, I have often forgotten to give control to the Lord. But when I've yielded my life to Him, I've been changed and the fruit has begun to grow in my life.

When we accept Jesus as our Savior, we begin the greatest adventure of our lives: becoming like Him! Others will see a picture of Christ by our example, especially when the fruit of the Holy Spirit has been formed within us. When He produces self-control in us, we see our situation clearly, control our emotions and actions, and allow Him to guide us in handling the situation correctly. Living a Spirit-filled life means living in perfect harmony with the life that God intended us to live—and bearing fruit that will last! —*John Ausmus*

1. In what areas of your life do you need more self-control?

2. How do you react when confronted?

3. What can you do today to allow the Holy Spirit to make you more like Christ?

Scripture: 1 Corinthians 9:24-27; Galatians 6:1-5; 2 Peter 1:3-11

Prayer: *Gracious God, thank You for continuing the good work You've begun in me and for producing fruit in my life that points others to Jesus! In His name, amen.*

Mourning into Dancing

You turned my lament into dancing;
You removed my sackcloth and clothed me
with gladness, so that I can sing to
You and not be silent. Lord my God,
I will praise You forever.
PSALM 30:11-12

One of the Division 1 schools in my area entered its conference tournament as the number eight seed and appeared to be a long shot to win it all. The head coach for the team admitted they fell short of expectations, but that the one goal they could hold on to was winning a conference tournament championship.

Despite the odds, the team achieved that goal by knocking off the first-, second- and fourth-seeded teams, earning an automatic berth in the NCAA tournament in the process. As one player said, the team put it together when it counted most.

We all know that falling short of our expectations can bring about many disappointments on and off the court. However, if we, like this team, keep looking forward to even a small hope of success, we'll often be glad we made the effort.

King David knew this firsthand. Although he had been chosen by God to lead the Israelites, he faced many struggles. But when he cried out to God and clung to the hope found in Him, David's mourning turned into dancing.

The Son of David, Jesus Christ, experienced far greater trials when He came to Earth. He endured the cross, submitting Himself to God for the joy that was set before Him (see Hebrews 12:2). He also knew that the mourning would soon be turned to dancing!

Likewise, God sometimes gives us a new outlook in difficult situations so that we might endure them (see 2 Corinthians 12:7-9), or He relieves us entirely by removing us from the situation (see Exodus 6:6). Whatever the circumstance, because of God's love and faithfulness, we can submit ourselves to Him, thankful that His joy is our strength!

Although we may not always be certain of how or when God will relieve us, as we seek Him in the midst of our daily challenges, we can always be certain that He will. —*Josh Carter*

1. What is one struggle in sports that you have been brought out of?

2. How can trials be beneficial?

3. How have you seen God turn sorrow into joy in your life?

Scripture: Ecclesiastes 3:1-4; Isaiah 61:1-3; Jeremiah 31:4

Prayer: *Lord, be the reason that I dance and sing today so that I might praise You forever! Amen.*

Rejoice in the Lord always.
I will say it again: Rejoice!
PHILIPPIANS 4:4

Athletics are full of emotion. Excitement, enthusiasm, disappointment, happiness and joy are all part of the competitive experience. Paul reminded Christians at Philippi to rejoice in the Lord, and the message is the same for us today. But we live in a difficult world with real battles. As John 10:10 tells us, "A thief comes only to steal and to kill and to destroy." What is the thief after? Not anything that can be seen in the physical—no, he wants to steal the joy in our hearts.

We must recognize, though, that happiness is not the same as joy. Happiness is a direct result of what happens in our lives. Joy comes as a result of trusting that God has everything under control. His Word tells us that when we acknowledge Him and trust in Him, we'll experience a peace that surpasses all understanding (see Philippians 4:7). God knows what we need. He guides our steps—our happiness and our joy—despite what the world and our trials try to tell us. The Lord uses each difficult situation to help bring us to the next level and increase our trust in Him

But John 10:10 also tells us that Jesus came in order that we might have life—and have it in abundance. In fact, He offered His own life in death so that we might live each day fully and abundantly with Him! That abundance is not about money but is found in the joy that results in knowing that, no matter what, He loves us and will use each experience in our lives to fulfill His purposes.

As coaches, we're filled with joy when we believe that God is at work in our lives, even if we might not see it in the physical. Because God is trustworthy and faithful, we can join Paul in rejoicing in the Lord always! When we do, our hearts are filled with an abundant life that no thief can ever steal! —*Lisa Phillips*

1. What brings you joy and happiness?

2. How would you define "abundant life"?

3. How can you develop the fruit of joy more
   fully in your life?

Scripture: Psalm 37:3-4; Proverbs 3:5-6; Jeremiah 29:10-14; John
10:7-18

Prayer: *I pray, Lord, that Your joy would spill over into all areas of my life so
that others might experience Your life in Jesus! Amen.*

Our Identity in Christ

Since, then, you have been raised with Christ,
set your hearts on things above, where
Christ is seated at the right hand of God.
Set your mind on things above, not
on earthly things.
COLOSSIANS 3:1-2, *NIV*

As coaches, whenever we are asked, "How are you?" we often reply
in terms of our team: "We struggled early but regrouped late in the
season."

Unfortunately, it's far too easy for us as coaches to become consumed with our team's performance. When we allow this to happen,
who we are can get lost amid the pressure to win. Learning to separate
athletic expectations from our true identity in Christ is an ongoing
and significant challenge.

As followers of Christ, we are not to lose sight of what matters most in this life. In Paul's letter to the Christians in the city of Colossae, he voiced concerns about the distractions of the time and their inherent dangers. He issued a warning to the Colossians (and to us) to pay attention and to be on guard because this world can be a captivating place.

Paul knew that this world's temporal rewards beckon with a fierce and determined strength. And just as the false teachings were attractive to the misguided Colossians, so can a winning record be equally alluring to a coach!

If we become ensnared by the rewards and attention inherent in success, we make ourselves vulnerable to the idolatrous practices that Paul warned against. Focusing our lives on anything but those "things above" is a recipe for failure. We will continually be disappointed and feel a loss of hope and will look to the next season or next recruit to fulfill us.

Paul is clear: Nothing of human design should become the focal point in our lives, even something as seemingly noble as leading a team to a successful season. Anything that stands in the way of our relationship with Christ keeps us from fully surrendering our hearts and minds to Him. And only He can satisfy our longings! —*Cheryl Baird*

1. Can you separate who you are in Christ from your team's performance?

2. What will it take for you to set your mind on "things above"?

3. What does it mean for you to surrender your team to God?

Scripture: Psalm 26:2-3; Philippians 3:7-20; Colossians 2:8

Prayer: *God, I want to find my whole identity in You! Please help me release the desire to replace You with anything that is of this world. Amen.*

The one who has My commandments and keeps
them is the one who loves Me. And the one who loves
Me will be loved by My Father. I also will love him
and will reveal Myself to him.

JOHN 14:21

In the ancient Middle East, there were three main ways to obtain water. The first was by digging a well. The second meant carving out a cistern. But the third way came naturally and did not require hard work or human energy: through the earth! A spring of water sometimes bubbled to the surface. Often in Scripture, that spring became a picture of God's grace and provision. Jesus told the woman at the well that the water He gives will become "a spring of water welling up to eternal life" (John 4:14, *NIV*). He also said, "Whoever believes in me, as the Scripture has said, streams of living water will flow from within him" (John 7:38, *NIV*).

When we devote ourselves to something—our coaching, our families, our sport or our church—we often find ourselves giving out of the spring within us. Sometimes that spring runs dry because we're trying to draw water from our own broken cisterns. Or sometimes we get exhausted digging for water in the wrong place. But when we allow God to be our source, His Spirit flows from within us, producing grace as we interact with other people.

From the well of Christ's living water flows a sense of deep respect for people and their positions. Because of our respect for them, we want to please them. We enjoy being around them. They motivate us to excellence by their example and bring out our best efforts. Imagine, then, what happens when we devote ourselves to the greatest person who ever lived, who emptied Himself for our sake! Everything else seems to fall into place.

Devotion to God means spending time with Him, drinking from His eternal well and loving Him by obeying His Word. When we do, our thirst will always be satisfied! —*Al Schierbaum*

1. What motivates you?

2. What does being devoted mean?

3. To whom or to what are you devoted?

Scripture: Isaiah 40:12-31; Matthew 6:9-15; John 14:21-23

Prayer: *Living Water, You alone satisfy all of my longings! Forgive me for trying to draw water from my own abilities. Turn me back to Your well today so that others, too, may drink of You! Amen.*

You Are What You Think

Finally, brothers, whatever is true, whatever is honorable, whatever is just, whatever is pure, whatever is lovely, whatever is commendable— if there is any moral excellence and if there is any praise—dwell on these things.

PHILIPPIANS 4:8

Almost every Christian coach I know wants to have a philosophy of coaching that is positive. But in the battle of competition, sometimes we get caught up in the heat of the moment and lose our focus. We may stay positive on the outside, but inside we are feeling the tension—tension that causes us to lose that positive edge.

I have found that what we *tell* our athletes to think about is exactly what they *will* think about. We may say, "Don't ever miss a serve on game point." What are they thinking when they come to the line? They are thinking about *not* missing the serve. What do they see? *Missing the serve,* which is exactly what we told them to think about!

Instead, in the same way Paul instructs us to "dwell on these things," we need to encourage our players to focus on the good and right and true ways to compete. This way, they are not thinking about anything else. We can coach our players to do exactly what we want for them by not bringing in anything that will cause them to lose their focus. Jesus is the perfect example of this: He was so single-minded in His purpose on Earth that He never wavered. He completely fulfilled the task that He had been given to do: go to the cross for our sake!

Paul says in Philippians to keep our minds *dwelling* on what is true, pure and excellent. When we do, our athletes will fulfill their goals and develop their gifts—and we will experience God's peace.
—*Kathie Woods*

1. Do you spend more time dwelling on the positives or the negatives?

2. How does your focus affect your life and professional goals?

3. What are the honorable, just, pure, commendable and praiseworthy things in your life?

Scripture: Psalm 119:97; Romans 12:2; Philippians 4:1-9

Prayer: *Thank You, Lord, for renewing my mind in Christ and redirecting my focus to be centered on Your grace! Amen.*

> As coaches, we need to encourage our players to focus on the good and right and true ways to compete.

Dear friends, we are God's children now, and what we will be has not yet been revealed. We know that when He appears, we will be like Him, because we will see Him as He is. And everyone who has this hope in Him purifies himself just as He is pure.

1 JOHN 3:2-3

Teresa was one of those athletes who was all spirit, gifted with more determination than natural talent. But her Christian faith and love for soccer had a powerful effect on my other public high school players. If I needed a surge of enthusiasm to flow through my team, I looked to Teresa.

During a difficult practice one day, Teresa struggled to finish a long-distance run. As I jogged to the end of the line to encourage her, she glanced upward and shouted, "Take me now, Lord Jesus! Take me now so I don't have to finish!" We both laughed so hard that we were through running in no time!

Though funny at the time, over the years I've often thought of her plea. Teresa instinctively knew that there was something far better in life than earthly struggles or physical pain. She knew that she was one of God's children and that something greater than this life awaited her: the hope of heaven.

When the apostle John wrote of such hope, he had firsthand experience. An eyewitness to the death of our Lord Jesus on the cross, John must have been crushed by the pain of such an event. But then he witnessed the resurrected Lord, the one who conquered death, appear to several hundred witnesses and then be taken up to heaven. John's hope sustained him during days of great persecution; it purified him and empowered him to live in expectation of Christ's return.

For coaches who want their players to experience God's love, there's no greater gift we can give than the hope of eternal life, the expectation that we will see Jesus as He is! Teresa reminded me of that hope at soccer practice, and her words still challenge us to keep looking forward to that amazing day! —*Jo Kadlecek*

1. What do you imagine heaven to be like?

2. How can hope sustain you today?

3. What does it mean to be "God's child now"?

Scripture: 1 Corinthians 15:3-8,17-18; Revelation 1:4-7

Prayer: *Risen Lord, may our contemplation of the gift of eternal life renew our love for You today! Amen.*

Some Winning Advice . . . Guaranteed

I have told you these things, so that in me you may have peace. In this world you will have trouble. But take heart! I have overcome the world.

JOHN 16:33, *NIV*

Trouble often seems to be waiting around every corner of daily life, especially for coaches. Whether it is a troubled player, an unfair referee, a nagging parent or an unreasonable principal, coaches can count on difficulties. They come with the territory!

Thankfully, Jesus never pretended that life would be a luxury cruise. "You will have trouble," He told His disciples. In fact, difficulties are guaranteed, an inevitable part of living in a fallen world. Jesus didn't deliver the trouble; He just knew it was coming.

Consequently, the best advice that we could heed—and give to others—is not to strive for a trouble-free practice or season. Nobody has that. Rather, in the midst of consuming troubles, Jesus invites us to experience the peace of His presence. Because it comes from the Master, such advice is foolproof, but the application of this truth is still up to us.

Jesus told His followers that real and lasting peace would come when we walk with Him. And He offered this advice before He went to the cross! He had not yet conquered the world. Still, He guaranteed this ahead of time because He knew that the "punishment for our peace was on Him" (Isaiah 53:5).

Coaching may seem to be about victories, which are important, but real victory comes when we battle through the troubles alongside Jesus. If we want to win any contest, we must seek Him to find peace! If we have no peace, it's because we have no Jesus. But if we know Jesus, we know peace, regardless of what troubles come our way! —*Clay Elliot*

1. What trouble have you experienced lately?

2. Are you experiencing peace in the midst of this trouble?

3. Will you heed the winning advice and seek peace today by walking with Jesus?

Scripture: Psalms 32; Isaiah 53:5; Philippians 3:1-11

Prayer: *Father, I admit that I don't like it when trouble comes my way, but I am grateful that You gave Your Son so that I could experience peace in the midst of my troubles. Swallow me up in Your peace as I submit to walking with You. In Jesus' name I live and pray, amen!*

> The Lord is a refuge for the oppressed, a refuge in times of trouble. Those who know Your name trust in You because You have not abandoned those who seek You, Lord.
>
> Psalm 9:9-10

Love is patient; love is kind. Love does not envy;
is not boastful; is not conceited; does not act improperly;
is not selfish; is not provoked; does not keep a record of
wrongs; finds no joy in unrighteousness, but rejoices
in the truth; bears all things, believes all things,
hopes all things, endures all things.

1 CORINTHIANS 13:4-7

During a recent NFL game, I watched as two future Hall of Fame coaches took the field. The announcers shared how they had talked with a player who had played for both coaches and asked him what was the difference between the two coaching styles. The player said that one coached by fear, the other by love. When asked what the player preferred, he shared that both can be effective, but that love lasts forever.

Christ coached a team of men as well. He easily could have used fear as a motivator to get them to do what He wanted them to do. He might have even been successful at it. But He chose a different path. He chose love. Better yet, He lived love. He was love! When Paul penned the "love chapter" in 1 Corinthians, he must have been thinking of Christ the entire time. As you read the passage, you can easily put in Jesus' name as a substitute for the word "love."

Coaching requires wisdom, understanding and discernment in knowing when to love and listen to your team. A coach who leads by fear will have success at times, but in the end he will lose respect and players will play to spite him or her. A coach who leads by love will gain not only respect but also admiration. He or she will build life-long relationships with players who know that they are loved.

One way to know if a coach leads by fear tactics is whether he or she cares more about the player or program than the person. The coach who leads by love always will care more about the person than the player. There is a huge difference. —*Jere Johnson*

1. As a coach, how do you fare when you substitute your name into the above verses from 1 Corinthians 13:4-7?

2. What is your greatest challenge as a coach?

3. Do your players know that you care about who they are as individuals?

Scripture: Matthew 22:34-39; John 13:34-35

Prayer: *Lord, help me to care more about the person than the player and show my players the love that I have for them. Amen.*

Cheerleaders or Critics

Therefore since we also have such a great cloud of witnesses surrounding us . . . Consider Him who endured such hostility from sinners against Himself, so that you won't grow weary and lose heart.
HEBREWS 12:1,3

A few years ago, I was privileged to participate in the memorial service of a man who was a faithful servant, dear friend, and former head football coach. Over 2,000 of this man's family, friends, colleagues and student-athletes attended the service.

As I stepped into the pulpit of the church, I thought, *Look at all these people. The grandstands are packed for him today.* Everyone *here is a cheerleader! What a great send-off for a coach—and a great testimony to a life well lived!*

As we experience the world of athletics, we'll find people cheering or booing, depending on the circumstances of the moment.

When we step into the spiritual realm, we read about that heavenly stadium filled with that "great cloud of witnesses," those great saints and heroes of the faith, encouraging and cheering us, God's earthly team, to victory. Imagine them applauding, yelling for us to finish the course, to fight the fight, to run the race, to keep the faith! They are *shouting* for us to run with perseverance, to fix our eyes on Jesus and to remember that, as bad as we may think our circumstances are, Jesus' circumstances, for our sake, were far worse.

The heroes of the faith exhort and cheer us on so that we won't forget how Jesus endured the cross, its shame and the hostility of humankind. They call out to us so that we won't grow weary and lose heart! As we go through our days today, we might experience both critics and cheerleaders. But we can't let them distract us from our Savior and that heavenly host of fans who've "got our backs"—no matter what the circumstances dictate! —*Jim Faulk*

1. In your daily life, who are your critics? Who are your cheerleaders?

2. How do you react to their responses?

3. What could you do today to hear the heavenly cheerleaders' shouts over the jeers of earthly critics?

Scripture: Psalm 20:7-8; Isaiah 43:2-3; Hebrews 12:1-3

Prayer: *Great God and Father, thank You that I am never alone in this race. Help me to cheer others on as together we fix our eyes on Jesus! Amen.*

> As we experience the world of athletics, we'll find people cheering or booing, depending on the circumstances of the moment.

> Then He said to them all, "If anyone wants to
> come with Me, he must deny himself, take up
> his cross daily, and follow Me."
>
> LUKE 9:23

When I was hired as the new offensive coordinator of the Houston/Tennessee Oilers in 1997, I knew that we had big challenges ahead. The Oilers had never made that exciting trip to the Super Bowl, so when the owners moved the team to Tennessee, it signaled a serious intention to reach new heights.

Our road to the Super Bowl was only possible through the grace of God, which motivated the unselfish attitudes of a group of players and coaches who considered the needs of the team more important than their own individual needs. While at training camp that season, we discovered several effective principles for building a championship team. These same principles can be applied to our lives as Christians as well, if we're willing to think beyond ourselves and dedicate our lives to the bigger purpose of God.

One of these guiding principles was communication. Most NFL summer training camps are hot, so we decided to use the weather to guide our communication and make sure it was "hot" as well: Honest, Open and Transparent. Since one of our main challenges that year was convincing a group of people from all walks of life to lose themselves for the sake of one cause, our communication also had to be effective.

The same is true, of course, for Christians. Every day, Christ invites us to lose ourselves for the sake of the single purpose of living for Him because He did the same for us! When we try to hide things from Him or from our brothers and sisters in Christ, we only create broken relationships and mistrust. In order to produce unity, we must promote truth. That means honestly pursuing Him, denying ourselves for the sake of others and transparently taking up His cross for all to see! —*Les Steckel*

1. How do you inspire your players to lose themselves for the sake of one cause?

2. How have you demonstrated an unselfish attitude toward your players? Toward your colleagues? Toward your family?

3. In what areas of your life do you need to be more H.O.T.?

Scripture: Mark 8:34-37; Philippians 2:1-4; James 3:14-18

Prayer: *Lord, may the words of my mouth and the meditations of my heart be pleasing to You today and helpful to others! Amen.*

Little Things

> His master replied, "Well done, good and faithful servant! You have been faithful with a few things; I will put you in charge of many things. Come and share your master's happiness!"
>
> MATTHEW 25:21, *NIV*

One of my favorite things about John Wooden's coaching was that he taught his players each year to put on their socks and tie their shoes properly. You'd think college-aged athletes could already do this, but Wooden took nothing for granted. He paid attention to the little things, which made the big things come more easily for his teams over the years.

Of course, Coach Wooden wanted to teach his players a lesson: If they were going to play in his program, they had to put aside what they wanted to do and follow his plans for the team. That discipline in the small things gave his teams great results, as they won 10 national championships and set an example for the rest of us how the little things make the biggest difference.

Sometimes, in walking with the Lord, we neglect what we might perceive as "the little things" because we get too busy. We forget that setting aside daily time with God in His Word, spending time in prayer, or serving our loved ones all help us learn to be faithful. But like the parable in Matthew's Gospel teaches us, we can't assume that we'll be given many things until we're first faithful with the few. These seemingly small steps make a huge difference in how we'll handle bigger responsibilities.

To serve the Lord, we must put aside our own selfish desires and follow Christ in the little things. After all, Scripture says that Jesus gave up His position as God to endure life as a man:

> [He] made himself nothing, taking the very nature of a servant, being made in human likeness . . . He humbled himself and became obedient to death—even death on a cross (Philippians 2:7-8, *NIV*).

As a result of His willingness to serve faithfully, God exalted Him and gave Him the name above all names: Jesus! —*Jere Johnson*

1. What little things can you do to help your team?

2. What small steps can you take toward faithfulness in your spiritual walk?

3. How can you be faithful in all areas of your life?

Scripture: Luke 16:10-12; Philippians 2:5-11; 1 Thessalonians 5:14-18

Prayer: *Thank You, God, for Your faithful love toward me and for helping my attitude today be like Christ's! Amen.*

> Do what you have learned and received and heard and
> seen in me, and the God of peace will be with you.
> PHILIPPIANS 4:9

We've all said it: The secret to success is practice, practice, practice. Sometimes we'll put the word "perfect" in front of all of those "practices" to nail down an even more effective plan. We all know that without practice we'll never reach the level of play that we desire.

When I was in high school, I trusted my coaches completely, so I practiced whatever they told me to. I desired success, which helped me to listen to them and heed their advice. In the same way, when we read that Paul urges us to "do what you have learned and received and heard and seen in me," we would be wise to heed his advice. A quick scan of the context reveals some of what Paul would want us to put into practice:

- Philippians 4:4—We should rejoice in the Lord.
- Philippians 4:5—Our gentleness should be evident (*NIV*).
- Philippians 4:6—We should pray about everything.
- Philippians 4:8—We should think about the good stuff.

As coaches, we could integrate these four ideas daily by rejoicing not just in winning but in practice or tough defeats; leading our players with gentleness as the Lord leads us; praying for our players and for every decision, from game plans to practice sessions; and filling our minds by meditating on God's goodness and promises.

Only when we put these Christlike attributes into practice with His help will we have the reserves to see the good when difficult circumstances arise. As we do, our faith in Him will be deepened and our Christian lives will become more authentic. In other words, we'll learn more of what it means to be "real" coaches. We'll become more like the people that God always intended us to be through Jesus Christ our Lord as we practice, practice, practice with Him! —*Clay Elliot*

1. What are the attributes of a "real" coach?
2. How do those characteristics compare with your coaching style?
3. What are some things that you could put into practice with God's help?

Scripture: Psalm 111:1-10; Philippians 4:1-9; 1 Timothy 4:11-16

Prayer: *Thank You, Lord, that You hear my prayers and fill me with Your joy and gentleness. I ask for Your wisdom today as I reflect Your glory and grace to each person that You bring across my path. Amen.*

The Power of Fear

If you really carry out the royal law prescribed in Scripture, You shall love your neighbor as yourself, you are doing well.

JAMES 2:8

Coach Smith was aware that one of his players was smoking pot. There was good evidence that he had even smoked on a team trip, which was clearly a violation of team rules. But Coach Smith did not take any action or even talk with the player.

At the end of the season, the principal called Coach Smith in for a meeting and told him that there was verifiable evidence the player had consistently violated team rules. The principal also had clear evidence that Coach Smith had known about it. Consequently, the coach was asked to resign.

Why had Coach Smith been unwilling to confront his player? There are lots of possibilities. The team was winning; the player had no other violations and came from a good family. There may have been many reasons, but it is likely that the main reason at the core of all of this was fear.

Fear can paralyze our willingness to act and do the right thing. It is certainly okay to feel afraid—that's part of being human. But when we allow fear to affect our ability to take appropriate action, we hurt others as well as ourselves.

First John 4:18 tells us, "Perfect love drives out fear." This Scripture clearly illustrates the conflict between love and fear. We cannot act out of fear and love at the same time. And we know from Jesus—whose obedient life and death was out of love for us—that the greatest commandment is to love!

As the next verse, 1 John 4:19, tells us, "We love because He first loved us." Because God loves us, we can love our players. And that means we cannot ignore their problems or pretend they don't exist. Instead, His love for us gives us the courage to do what's right! —*Bill Burnett*

1. What situations in life create fear for you?

2. How do you naturally respond to the realization that you will have to confront someone?

3. What is "perfect love"?

Scripture: 2 Kings 17:35-36; Psalm 27:1-6; Isaiah 17:7-8; 1 John 14:13-21

Prayer: *Lord, thank You for loving me with a perfect love. Help me to reflect that love to those people whom You've put in my life. In Christ's name, amen.*

> Fear can paralyze our willingness to act and do the right thing.

> So because of Christ, I am pleased in weaknesses,
> in insults, in catastrophes, in persecutions, and in
> pressures. For when I am weak, then I am strong.
> 2 CORINTHIANS 12:10

Many of us learned the "Jesus Loves Me" song as children, but the last part always bothered me: "Jesus loves me! This I know, for the Bible tells me so. Little ones to Him belong; They are weak but He is strong."[6] To me, displaying weakness seemed to contradict the very goal of competition.

As I was learning to compete in athletics, the idea of embracing weakness seemed ridiculous. I thought that I had to renounce all that I had learned in the gym in order to become weak. I mean, who has ever been chosen for a team for being the weakest player? Who breaks into a starting lineup because she is weaker than her teammates? I wanted to be strong and display that power for anyone who cared to watch.

So, as coaches who teach athletes to be stronger than their opponents, can we display weakness of any kind and still model a competitive and driven spirit? I've learned that the answer is yes. It starts with the reality that we find true freedom in Christ when we believe our weakness is an asset. When we admit our weakness to God, we rely on Him rather than on our own abilities. We are truly powerful when we become fully dependent on Him. In fact, becoming weak is a gift that better equips us to serve Him. In the process, we become more like Christ, who became weak on the cross for our sakes, that we might be strong in Him. This is weakness that leads to strength.

To be "pleased in weaknesses" is a call to surrender to our Creator, to allow Him to reign in our beings and to take hold of our hearts. He has given us every gift we possess—even the gift of weakness—as an opportunity to honor His name, not ours. —*Cheryl Baird*

1. What stirs in your heart when you think about showing weakness?

2. What keeps you from turning over every gift to the Lord?

3. How is God asking you to rely more on Him?

Scripture: Psalm 121; Romans 8:26; Philippians 4:13

Prayer: *Lord, teach me how to embrace my weaknesses and use every gift that You've given me for Your purposes. Amen.*

Time-Out

But God proves His own love for us in that while we were still sinners Christ died for us!
ROMANS 5:8

The time-out. What a great tool! When you realize that your athletes are becoming unnerved, out of breath and in need of a break, a time-out is a great way to stop, reenergize, refocus, reward and reassure them. Something as simple as a water break time-out to reenergize your team is all it takes to get them going again. In the same way, our "thirst" for God requires that we take time-outs in our lives in order to be reenergized by our Coach, Jesus Christ.

Sometimes we call a time-out to refocus because the other team threw something at us that we weren't expecting. It's like that in life too. Things happen that are out of our control. We're upset by the events of the moment and lose our focus. The way to get our focus back is to keep our eyes on Christ.

Other times we call a time-out to just rest in the moment and reward our team for a job well done. God desires to do that for us. One day, we may hear those awesome words from the Master Coach: "Well done, good and faithful servant."

Sometimes we are in a hopeless situation and need to call a time-out to reassure our team. If our athletes realize that they have meaning and purpose in life, they will run through "brick walls" for us, because they know that we care about them. God seeks to reassure us in the same way. We are truly free to run through any of the brick walls in our lives, because of the power of His Love for us—"that while we were still sinners Christ died for us!"

God is our Coach. We need time-outs so that we can listen to what He has to say. If we're obedient to His calling, He can set a pace for us so that we don't get run-down or lose focus or faith. We can rest in Him and know that He is God. —*Donalyn Knight*

1. How do you know when you need to take a time-out?

2. Is your alone time with God a top priority?

3. What changes do you need to make in your own schedule to allow for a time-out with God?

Scripture: Romans 8:28-39; 1 Corinthians 9:24-26; Galatians 6:7-9

Prayer: *Dear Lord, help me to set aside time to meet with You in prayer. Remind me often that time-outs are good for the soul, not just the body. In Jesus' name, amen.*

> Those who trust in the Lord will renew their strength; they will soar on wings like eagles; they will run and not grow weary; they will walk and not faint.
>
> Isaiah 40:31

> Then Abram said to Lot, "Please, let's not
> have quarreling between you and me, . . . since
> we are relatives. Isn't the whole land before you?
> Separate from me: if [you go] to the left,
> I will go to the right; if [you go] to
> the right, I will go to the left."
>
> GENESIS 13:8-9

In his 16 years as the coach of the Boston Celtics, Red Auerbach guided his team to 9 NBA Championships. He retired after the 1966 season as the winningest coach in NBA history with 938 wins.

While his teams had some great players, they were characterized more by their team play, which included a new concept of using role players. "That's a player who willingly undertakes the thankless job that has to be done in order to make the whole package fly," Auerbach said.[7]

In the Bible, Abraham and his nephew Lot were also a team. But as they traveled together with their flocks, herds and households, they realized that the land could not support them both. The result was strife among their people.

Rather than flaunt his role as the leader, Abraham gave Lot his choice of land. Abraham could have looked out for himself and his household, but instead he sacrificed his desires for the good of his people and trusted God to provide what they needed.

In the same way, Christ gave up His authority by going to the cross, and we, too, can reflect such sacrifice as we serve others. It's not easy to come off the bench, but like Auerbach recognized, unselfish players off the bench are just as important to the success of a team as the starters. Christian competitors have a great opportunity to serve their teams by being willing to give up their place. In fact, those who want to be great on their teams recognize the joy of serving as Christ did! —*Josh Carter*

1. How can you encourage attitudes of service, rather than selfishness, on your team?

2. How have you seen selfless competitors influence a team?

3. What one thing can you do today to reflect a selfless attitude toward your players?

Scripture: Matthew 20:25-28; 1 Corinthians 10:24; Philippians 2:3-4; Hebrews 11:25-26

Prayer: *Lord Jesus, thank You for Your life of sacrifice. I pray that You would increase that I may decrease as I serve others for Your glory! Amen.*

Big Me, Little Team

Everyone should look out not only for his own interests, but also for the interests of others.

PHILIPPIANS 2:4

I'll never forget standing in the locker room with my Division 1 field hockey players and listening to their postgame chatter. I was their new assistant coach, we had just lost our first game, and I was anxious to see how they were doing.

To my amazement, I didn't sense the usual sober mood that comes with losing. In fact, the team leaders were upbeat as they discussed their glory moments while they changed out of their uniforms.

One player, Maureen, talked about her personal stats, excited about her goal. Another player, Ellen, was happy with her two goals. None of the "superstars" cared about our injured fullback. I wanted to tell Ellen that if she'd only passed more we would have scored more and possibly won—but no one seemed interested. The team continued highlighting their own efforts. I walked out, bewildered.

As the season progressed, I realized that I wasn't coaching a team, but rather a group of individuals primarily concerned with personal success. Talented as they were, they never experienced the glory of a shared victory or the bond that comes from a hard-fought team loss. They had no idea that they could be better than the sum of all their parts.

When the head coach also focused on personal stats, a tone of selfishness was set and by the season's end, ours was a group of disillusioned women. After their last game, few seemed upset that the season was over.

Watching a group of gifted athletes lose game after game showed me how much is lost when we choose ourselves over the team. I can only wonder what the women on the team would have been like if they had decided instead to live as Christ—the one who washed Peter's feet, served lunch to 5,000 and, ultimately, took our place on the cross.

His life, death and resurrection remind us that the call to serve others is the greatest victory we can ever experience! —*Eileen F. Sommi*

1. In what ways can you model Christ's service to others on your team?

2. How do you coach a selfish player?

3. How can you "live as Christ" today?

Scripture: Romans 12; 1 Corinthians 12; Philippians 2:14-17

Prayer: *Jesus, fill me with Your Spirit that I might love others more than myself. Amen.*

Come to Me, all you who are weary and
burdened, and I will give you rest.
MATTHEW 11:28

The life of a coach goes something like this: get up early, go to the office, teach class or watch film, talk with other coaches, go to a lunch meeting, prepare for team meetings, lead practice, follow up with coaches and players, and finally, head home. At home, the schedule is just as full: chat with family, make some calls, finish some chores and eat dinner.

Obviously, a coach's life is busy. How could anything more possibly fit into the day? But one thing often goes missing, something of vital and eternal importance. This is where "the squeeze" comes in.

The squeeze is the brief amount of time that we spend each day with Jesus. When we scan the day planner, we don't often see that 5 or 10 minutes listed. Then out of guilt or obligation, we give the Master Coach a little face time and squeeze in a few minutes with the One who first called us to coaching. As the season picks up, though, He gets squeezed out rather than squeezed in.

The squeeze is ever present. Life gets busy and overwhelming, and the One who can help us the most often doesn't get the opportunity. But Jesus waits, patiently. In Matthew's Gospel, Jesus says, "Come to me." He knows that we are tired and weary. He knows that we need a break. In fact, He became weak on the cross so that we might be strong and filled with Him. What greater proof is there that He wants to spend time with someone He loves—*you!*

Even when life's demands are pulling you in a million different directions, just remember that squeezing Him in is always better than squeezing Him out. Once He is in, listen, love and learn from the only Coach who can give us more than we ever imagined. The more we do, the more we'll want to make time with Him daily. —*Jere Johnson*

1. Are you squeezing the Lord in or out of your life?

2. What prevents you from making time for Him?

3. Why do you think it is important to squeeze in time with God each day?

Scripture: Psalm 23; Isaiah 40:27-31; Hebrews 12:2-3

Prayer: *Loving Father, thank You that You forgive me for the times that I forget You. Thank You for making a way, through Your Son, for me to come to You each day. Help me protect my time with You, Lord. Amen.*

Pressure Release

To the weak I became weak, in order to win the weak. I have become all things to all people, so that I may by all means save some. Now I do all this because of the gospel, that I may become a partner in its benefits.

1 CORINTHIANS 9:22-23

We entered summer league basketball with a young team. Our inexperienced guards struggled to get our offense working, especially against a high-pressure, man-to-man defense.

One day in practice, I tried a new strategy. I taught my players several pressure-release, back-door plays that changed our focus and took advantage of the defense. I told them that we would invite the pressure so that we could cut and score lay-ups. My players were skeptical.

In the next game, when the defense was zealous and our guards wide-eyed, I called a time-out to remind the team what we'd learned. Back on the court, still afraid, my players decided to try to execute the play. Our wing came toward the sideline, and then cut to the basket. Our point guard passed to her and she scored! The way the team celebrated, you'd have thought we had won a championship!

Sometimes, the toughest defenses that coaches face are the walls our players put up. We try to love and care for them, but they're not so sure of us. They ignore instruction from us on the court or field, cross their arms, avoid eye contact and dare us to connect with them. The harder we try, the tougher their defenses become. As coaches of such players, we need to master the back-door play.

Paul understood this and "became all things to all people . . . [to] save some." Because God came to Earth as man to reach us, He can help us find ways to release the pressure that our players might feel.

As we begin to understand how to reach our players in creative, back-door ways, the defenses will come down, and we can speak into their hearts the love of Christ! —*Debbie Haliday*

1. Do you expect your players to adjust to you, or do you sometimes adjust to them?

2. Do some players resist your coaching? Do you pray for them?

3. What are some specific "back door" strategies that you could add to your team's routine to help them get to know you better and trust you more?

Scripture: Isaiah 61; John 15:9-17; Acts 17:22-31

Prayer: *Father, please give me the creativity and energy I need to coach this generation of athletes for Your sake. In Jesus' name, Amen.*

Teach me Your way, Lord, and I will live by Your truth.
PSALM 86:11

One of my all-time favorite sports movies is the basketball classic *Hoosiers*. In one particular scene, Hickory High needed a sub, and the coach didn't have anyone to put in the game except Ollie, the manager. Ollie went in, immediately got fouled, and had to go to the line for two free throws. The crowd was yelling, the opposing team was taunting, and Ollie's knees were shaking as he stepped to the line.

Ollie nailed the first basket. Then, the opposing team called a time-out. Ollie's coach gathered his team together and told them that "*after* Ollie hits the free throw" they would run a certain defense. Because the coach was a voice of truth at that moment in Ollie's life, the unsuspecting player stepped up and hit the next free throw. And his team won!

Throughout the Bible, we see stories of men and women who heard voices of opposition but chose to listen to the voice of truth. What if Joshua had listened to those who said they only needed to march around Jericho six times? What if David had believed those who said that he was too young to defeat Goliath? What if Esther had not gone to the king to intervene on behalf of her people?

Surely, the outcome of each situation would have been tragic if they had not listened to the voice of God pouring truth into their lives. And hundreds of years later, that same voice fulfilled the promises of their lives when Jesus appeared on the scene and the voice said, "This is My beloved Son . . . Listen to Him!" (Matthew 17:5).

We all have voices of opposition in our lives. Satan wants us to listen to them and fail. However, one voice rings louder and truer than any other: God's voice found in His Son and in His Word! —*Jere Johnson*

1. Are you listening to the right voice?

2. Whose voice do you hear in your life today?

3. How can you spend more time in the Word or in prayer to better hear the voice of truth?

Scripture: Psalms 29:3-4; 66:18-20; Mark 9:1-13; John 18:28-38

Prayer: *Living Word, thank You that You never stop speaking to me through prayer and the Bible. I ask that You would give me ears to hear Your voice all day long! Amen.*

Doing the Right Thing

For am I now trying to win the favor of people,
or of God? Or am I striving to please people?
If I were still trying to please people,
I would not be a slave of Christ.

GALATIANS 1:10

Marquette's football team was 10-0 heading into the final game of the season, and it appeared that the program would soon have its first championship. But a few days before the game, the coach received a call: 16 of his starters had been arrested for underaged drinking! Team rules dictated alcohol use as punishable by suspension. The next week, the coach watched his team's hopes evaporate in a 63-0 loss as 16 of his regular starters stood on the sidelines.

The coach would likely have found support had he imposed a gentle slap on the wrist for his guilty players. Certainly, many coaches overlook such offenses or wait until after the season to enforce discipline. This coach, however, made a difficult decision and placed more importance on citizenship, integrity and character than on winning a football game. In a society in which the indiscretions of athletes are often overlooked, this coach's firm commitment is certainly admirable!

Christians are frequently faced with similar decisions. Often, doing the right thing is not the easiest, most popular or most rewarding course of action. Society suggests that it's okay to tell little lies, fudge the numbers or break commitments. While these actions may make life easier or lead to short-term benefits, they erode our integrity.

Doing the right thing may not always be applauded, but that doesn't mean we should avoid it. Why? Because Jesus Christ set the standard for us. When brought before Pilate, who had the power to decide His fate, Christ could have denied who He was or escaped with His life. Instead, He faced the consequences of death for our sin! His grace, therefore, strengthens us to do what is right and please God, not people! —*Michael Wiggins*

1. In what areas of your life have you made ethical compromises?

2. How do you demonstrate integrity in your relationships?

3. How do you hold your players accountable for their actions?

Scripture: 1 Samuel 24:1-22; Daniel 3:8-30; Hosea 14:9

Prayer: *Lord, You are perfect in every way. Please reveal to me the areas in my life in which I am not doing the right things so that I may have an impact for Your kingdom. Amen.*

**Now faith is the reality of what is hoped for,
the proof of what is not seen.**

HEBREWS 11:1

After losing every soccer game and almost every basketball game in the past season, I was learning a lot about perseverance, or "doing the deal" no matter what. We all like to win, but it becomes harder for coaches and their players to keep going when they are on a losing streak. It's not easy to encourage players to win when they realistically don't have a chance.

Because I live in a "softball" town, most of our best athletes play for the leagues rather than the schools. We have no developmental soccer programs, so it's difficult to be competitive with other schools. I knew a recreational soccer league could help develop players, but many never expected that it would work in our town. Consequently, I wrestled in prayer about coaching, since it didn't look like I was doing the players any good.

Then God began to change things. Our city recreational director called to say that they would start "rec soccer." Then one of our athletes was offered a scholarship from a nearby college despite our losing season. Just when it looked like nothing good would come out of the year, God reminded me that He is always at work for the sake of His people, even when we're not sure what's happening. Just as the people wondered if anything good could come out of Nazareth (see John 1:46), so, too, does God continue to remind us that things are not always as they seem. No one expected the Savior of the world to die an excruciating death on a cross—but He did because He loves us!

By having faith in God and persevering in what we believe He is asking of us, we can watch Him take any situation and do something good. As one friend says, "Don't give up five minutes before the miracle!" —*Jenny Burgins*

1. Where in your life does it get hard to stay the course?

2. Are you walking by faith or by sight?

3. How do you know when the Holy Spirit is guiding you?

Scripture: 1 Corinthians 9:24; Philippians 3:13-14; 1 Timothy 6:11-12

Prayer: *Thank You, Lord, for teaching me to press on toward the goal of knowing You no matter how I feel. Help me to look for Your miracles! Amen.*

Making Courageous Choices

Haven't I commanded you: be strong and courageous? Do not be afraid or discouraged, for the Lord your God is with you wherever you go.

JOSHUA 1:9

Sometimes I wonder why it is so difficult for coaches to be still and listen. We have no problem knowing how to lead, direct others or give commands. But to whom do we look when we need direction? Who helps us make tough decisions?

We don't have to look far in Scripture to find a leader with similar challenges. Joshua was a brilliant military leader and had a strong spiritual influence, but his success came because he had learned whom to go to when he faced difficult choices. Joshua knew that unless he first submitted to God, he would never accomplish what he'd been given to do. So when God spoke, Joshua listened and obeyed.

Joshua's ability to submit to God teaches us about another leader who became the greatest man to ever walk the earth because of His sacrificial submission to God. Instead of being afraid, He faced an unjust judge; and instead of giving up, He endured an excruciating death on the cross.

Like Joshua, Jesus Christ knew that the greatest gift humankind could receive was the gift of God's presence. Yet He gave that up as well and endured separation from the Father through His death on the cross so that the Lord our God would be with us wherever we go.

How often as coaches have we been challenged to make choices that greatly influence the lives of those we love and lead? We all know it can be stressful making the right choices. Thankfully, we have a God who understands our anxieties, and because of Jesus' courage to choose death for our sake, He promises to be with us wherever we go! As we submit to His counsel, we'll gain the wisdom we need to make courageous choices. —*Larry Kerr*

1. What courageous decisions have you had to make?

2. How do you seek God's help in making your decisions?

3. How do you discern whether God is talking to you or you're responding to your own desires?

Scripture: Deuteronomy 31:6-8; Proverbs 3:2-6; Matthew 7:13-14

Prayer: *Father, thank You for Your promise to always be with me wherever I go. Help me to spend time in Your presence so that I will be strong and courageous for Your sake. Amen.*

> God—His way is perfect;
> the word of the Lord is pure.
> He is a shield to all who take refuge in Him.
>
> Psalm 18:30

Test yourselves to see if you are in the faith.
Examine yourselves. Or do you not recognize
for yourselves that Jesus Christ is in you?
—unless you fail the test.

2 CORINTHIANS 13:5

In 2003, LPGA golfer Annika Sorenstam became the first woman in 58 years to compete with men in a PGA tournament. Although she missed the cut by four shots, she had a respectable tournament and finished as well as or better than several of her competitors. "I tested myself from start to finish," she said afterward. "That's why I was here."[8] Sorenstam put herself to the test to find out just how good she was.

If we don't test ourselves, we will never know how strong we are. Paul's final words to the Corinthians serves as a wake-up call for us. In this challenge, he tells the Corinthians to test themselves to see whether they are Christians—to take an honest look at their lives to see if they are demonstrating faith in Jesus Christ through their actions.

Just because Annika Sorenstam didn't pass her test doesn't mean that she is no longer a true golfer. It just means that she had an unintentional setback. In the same way, just because we sin doesn't mean that we are not truly Christians. We all have setbacks with sin, but as Christians, our lifestyle should not be one characterized by willful, habitual sin.

As Sorenstam tested herself on the golf course, we too should examine ourselves to find out where we are in our relationship with Jesus Christ. Some "test" questions that might be helpful include: Are you a Christian? Have you turned away from sin and committed your life to Jesus Christ, trusting in Him alone for the forgiveness of sins and the gift of eternal life? Does your lifestyle give evidence of your faith in Jesus Christ? —*Josh Carter*

1. How did you answer the above "test" questions?

2. If you didn't pass the "test," what needs to happen next in your life? If you did pass, how are you demonstrating your faith in Christ?

3. What is one of the toughest tests that you have faced in competition?

Scripture: Psalm 139:23-24; 1 Thessalonians 5:12-22; 1 John 1:5-10

Prayer: *Almighty God, thank You that today I can walk in the freedom of forgiveness because of Jesus Christ. Amen.*

No Excuses

If I had not come and spoken to them, they would not be guilty of sin. Now, however, they have no excuse for their sin.

JOHN 15:22, *NIV*

I once worked with a head football coach who had a large sign behind his desk that simply read "No Excuses." What this meant to his staff and players was that he would not accept any explanations when something went wrong. He wanted them to be personally responsible and not put the blame on any other people or circumstances.

I see a lack of responsibility today on the part of athletes whenever their coaches call them to be accountable. The players tell their coach that they didn't hear the play, or they blame someone else for making a mistake. Nothing upsets a coach more than a player refusing to be accountable for his or her actions. And nothing is a worse role model to players than when a coach will not accept responsibility for his or her mistakes.

We can't make any excuses for our sin either. If we believe in Jesus Christ and know in our hearts that He lived a sinless life and died for us on the cross, then we must hate sin as much as He did. Why? Because sin prevents us from enjoying the presence of a holy God and from living the righteous life that He desires of us!

To allow ourselves to do what we know is wrong and then justify our actions is to give way to sin. Instead, we can live in the freedom of God's forgiveness by confessing our sins to Him and allowing His righteousness to shine through us so that others may see His love! —*Ken Kladnik*

1. Under what circumstances do you feel you need to make excuses?

2. How do you react when someone fails to take responsibility for his or her actions?

3. In what ways can you be more accountable?

Scripture: Psalm 51; Matthew 25:14-30; Luke 14:16-23; Romans 1:18-25

Prayer: *Lord, I pray that You will help me to be more obedient to You and to not make excuses for my sinful actions. I want to follow Jesus today, whose blood cleanses me from all unrighteousness so that I can live in Your grace and mercy. Amen.*

"It's important to accept our mistakes and learn from them. We cannot use them as excuses."
John Wooden

Whatever you ask in My name, I will do it, so that
the Father may be glorified in the Son. If you ask
Me anything in My name, I will do it.

JOHN 14:13-14

Why is asking so hard for some of us? Whether it's for a ride to the airport, a few dollars for lunch, or (better yet) financial support to take some athletes to FCA camp, many of us avoid asking like the plague.

Of course, there are times when even the most self-sufficient among us is willing to swallow all pride and plead before the "throne of grace." I have personally witnessed the amazing transformation of coaches, players and fans whose circumstances turned them into fervent prayer warriors. This phenomenon typically occurs during a game when their team is down by a point with a few ticks left on the clock and the least-talented shooter is on the free-throw line. Who among us hasn't uttered a prayer in times such as these?

Maybe it isn't a close game that brings us to our knees. Perhaps it is a life-altering event like the recovery of a loved one from illness or the safe return of a son or daughter from a tour of duty abroad. The truth is that we pray best when we are most helpless. We pray best when we are willing to come before God and admit our need. We pray best when, like little children, we set aside our pride and self-sufficiency and simply come before our Father with the desires of our hearts.

Jesus said, "Keep asking, and it will be given to you." The Son of God—who intimately knew about asking and giving–intentionally used the word "given" when He spoke to His followers. Not "lent." Not "sold." Not "leased." "Given," free of charge. Jesus didn't promise that we would be given exactly what we asked for, but He did say that we would receive. It costs us nothing to ask, but it cost Him everything to give! —*Kathy Malone*

1. What are some reasons why you don't ask for what you need?

2. When was the last time you felt helpless?

3. What is one desire of your heart that you can take to the Father right now?

Scripture: Romans 8:26; Ephesians 6:18; James 4:2

Prayer: *Heavenly Father, thank You that You invite me to ask! Help me to put aside my pride and come to You like a child full of wonder and in need of grace. Amen.*

I'm Tired . . . He's Not

Although my spirit is weak within me,
You know my way. Along this path I travel
they have hidden a trap for me.
PSALM 142:3

When David wrote this instructive psalm, he was in trouble. He was most likely cowering in a hole dug deeply into a hill, hiding from enemies that were pursuing him. He was lonely, desperate and in need of help.

As he hid from his adversaries, he felt out of control and uncertain of the future. So David implored the Lord for guidance, acknowledging in this time of distress that his trust and confidence had to come from God.

Many of us can echo David's cry in this psalm. As coaches, we often experience periods in a season when it feels like people are out to trap us, athletes are disinterested or uninvolved, and administrators are demanding wins.

The cyclical nature of coaching naturally can lead to feelings of inadequacy and insecurity. The rough times can be draining, leaving us feeling empty or without sufficient resources to survive another season, let alone another off-season.

But David teaches us from a dark cave that though we can only see this very moment, God can see the entire future. If we relinquish our desire to control our destiny, God promises to walk faithfully ahead of us and light the way.

He mercifully led the Israelites through the desert, and the same God who thousands of years ago lit their path desires that we call out to Him today. He promises to lead and guide us through the darkest of times.

We serve a God who came to Earth in the body of a man. Jesus experienced fatigue, felt the abandonment of those closest to Him, and was burdened by the self-serving demands of people. That's why Jesus understands our cries to Him in the midst of dark, lonely and tiring times! —*Cheryl Baird*

1. Have you ever felt like David when he was hiding in the cave?

2. Do you resist allowing God to take over when you feel tired?

3. Why do you think we often rely upon ourselves in time of distress?

Scripture: Psalm 107:1-9; Isaiah 2:5; 1 Peter 2:9

Prayer: *God Almighty, You alone can fill me with strength and grace today. I receive both from You now in Your faithful name! Amen.*

Do you not know that the runners in a stadium all race, but only one receives the prize? Run in such a way that you may win. Now everyone who competes exercises self-control in everything. However, they do it to receive a perishable crown; but we an imperishable one.

1 CORINTHIANS 9:24-25

Like most high school coaches, I had a goal to some day help an athlete win a state championship. As a former 800-meter runner, I wanted to help an athlete win that exact event. In my first season as a high school distance coach, achieving this goal became a possibility when one of my runners made it to the finals of the 800-meter at the state meet. But it was there that God taught me a valuable lesson.

I had expected to be at the finals in five or ten years, not in my very first year. But I also didn't expect to feel the emptiness that I felt as I watched my runner compete. I wondered if this was what coaching was all about. I remembered how much time had gone into training this one athlete as well as the time spent training my other athletes. I weighed that against how much time I'd committed to these athletes' personal and spiritual growth and quickly realized that I'd fallen into the trap that many coaches fall into: I'd made the product—the goal of winning—a higher priority than the process of shaping lives.

That day, I learned two things: (1) God is more concerned with how things are accomplished than with what is accomplished; and (2) God doesn't care about numbers as much as He cares about hearts—and He proved this to all humankind when He sent His only Son to Earth to take our sins to the cross.

As the gun went off that day, I decided that no matter the outcome, I would from that time forward be as much or more concerned with the spiritual training of my athletes than I was with their physical training! —*Toby C. Schwartz*

1. Are you more concerned with winning than you are with the growth your athletes?

2. What goals do you consider most important?

3. Does the process drive the goals, or do the goals drive the process?

Scripture: Ezekiel 11:17-21; Matthew 23:23-28; Luke 16:14-18

Prayer: *Thank You, Lord, that You've given me the privilege of caring for my athletes today. Help me to show them the imperishable crown that Jesus Christ offers to us! Amen.*

Focus

Climbing out of the boat, Peter started walking on the water and came toward Jesus. But when he saw the strength of the wind, he was afraid. And beginning to sink he cried out, "Lord, save me!" Immediately Jesus reached out His hand, caught hold of him, and said to him, "You of little faith, why did you doubt?"

MATTHEW 14:29-31

Homecoming week can strike fear into the heart of a coach. There's the dance, the pep assembly, the class competitions and, of course, the game, which is often the last to be mentioned. Although our players know better, all the festivities can distract them. It's a challenge to help them stay focused and arrive at the game ready to play. I admit, some seasons it causes *me* not to see straight.

Life pulls and tugs at us, which often causes us to become distracted, confused, overconfident or afraid. During these times, I'm reminded of the apostle Peter. Following Jesus' invitation to go to

Him on the water, Peter got out of the boat and actually walked to Him—on the water! At first he had no problem navigating his steps. Then he started sinking. What had changed? Only his focus. Instead of looking to Jesus, Peter shifted his attention to the water, the waves and the laws of gravity. But Christ did what He always does for those He calls: He reached out and saved Peter!

Most coaches I know are like Peter. We enter the profession wanting to make a difference in young people's lives by sharing the love of Jesus through athletics. We soon find, however, that our focus has shifted to our resumé, our team's winning percentage or the activities surrounding the game. We begin sinking because we have forgotten to keep our focus on Jesus.

Although *we* might be frustrated with our players during Homecoming week for losing their focus on the game, thankfully Jesus always waits for us to give Him the attention He deserves as our Savior and Lord. He is always ready to save us from drowning and to draw us to Himself! —*Bryan Wells*

1. What priorities define your life?

2. Do your priorities apply equally to your coaching life?

3. What grabs your attention away from Christ?

Scripture: Proverbs 17:24; Matthew 6:25-34; John 6:16-21

Prayer: *Lord, thank You that You perfect my faith. Draw me so close to You today that I am not distracted by the cares of the world. Amen.*

> It's a challenge to help our players stay focused and arrive at the game ready to play. Some seasons it causes me not to see straight.

**Now faith is the reality of what is hoped for,
the proof of what is not seen.**

HEBREWS 11:1

As the head women's basketball coach at the same institution for 26 years, I had just completed a rewarding season. We had a great group of athletes who played their hearts out, got along well and won games. There were many magical moments during the season, and no one wanted it to be over. But all good things must come to an end.

Like many coaches, I went through a period of letdown in which I needed to recharge for the next season. Though we'd just finished one season, a new one was around the corner. Thankfully, I had learned years before that what I enjoyed most about coaching was the process of preparing for "what is not seen." So even though I didn't know what tomorrow or the next season would bring, which recruits we'd need, or whether those recruits would blend well with the veterans, I knew that the unknowns at the end of a season didn't have to be unnerving. Instead, they could be exciting—*if* I had faith!

That's why I'm encouraged that "faith is the reality of what is hoped for." It energizes us. As coaches, we don't have to rely on ourselves, our players or our records. Instead, because Christ gave up His control by going to the cross for our sake, we can give up control and rely on Him. His peace is "the proof of what is not seen," regardless of the circumstances.

It quiets me to know that God is in control and that, win or lose, Christ has given me the faith to tackle another season and the hope that the best is yet to come! As we prepare for the unknowns of the next season (or even the next contest), we can rest in the assurance that Christ has filled us with His Holy Spirit, offering us hope for eternity and recharging us along the way! —*Susan Johnson*

1. How do you recharge between each season?

2. Do the unknowns of the future unnerve you or give you hope?

3. Has your faith in Christ enabled you to share an optimistic attitude with those around you?

Scripture: Jeremiah 14:22; Luke 12:22-31; Romans 12:12

Prayer: *Lord, increase my faith in You today. Thank You for the gift of peace in Jesus Christ. Amen.*

Holding On

Now you, man of God, run from these things;
but pursue righteousness, godliness, faith,
love, endurance, and gentleness. Fight the good
fight for the faith; take hold of eternal life, to
which you were called and have made a good
confession before many witnesses.

1 TIMOTHY 6:11-12

Those of us who watch a lot of sports programs on television have probably seen the St. Louis Cardinals' "blanket" commercial. It begins with a man who wraps a red St. Louis Cardinals' blanket around himself.

As it turns out, the blanket is the one constant in his life as he grows up. As a child, he uses it as a cape when he runs up the steps, and he drapes it over his bed when he studies. It is on the seat when he learns to play the drums as a teenager, in the trunk when he moves out of the house, and around his girlfriend while they watch a movie.

The commercial ends with the man wrapping the blanket around his child as these words come on the screen: "Without sports, what would we hold on to?"

For avid sports fans, the commercial seems to be suggesting that the one thing that we can count on is our sport or our team. As coaches, we try to help our team win. As fans, we cheer for our team like it's a matter of life and death. But for anyone who has professed Jesus Christ as his or her Lord and Savior, there is something far more fulfilling than sports.

Paul told Timothy to hold on to eternal life, because with Jesus Christ, he had been called into the most satisfying relationship that he would ever experience. The same is true for us! We hold on to Jesus Himself, acknowledging that He is the source of eternal life and the hope during every stage of our lives.

As Christian coaches, we can show our athletes and colleagues what we are holding on to by holding on first to Jesus and then wrapping His faithful love around our lives for others to witness! —*Alvin Cheng*

1. What are you holding on to in order to get through life?

2. How would the people in your life describe what you hold on to?

3. How can you hold on to Christ as you coach today?

Scripture: Psalm 119:30-32; Mark 7:6-8; 1 Thessalonians 5:12-22

Prayer: *Thank You, almighty God, that You have surrounded me with Your love and provided for me the gift of eternal life through Jesus Christ! Amen.*

Apply yourself to instruction and listen
to words of knowledge.

PROVERBS 23:12

A special tree grows each year in every sport. It's called the "coaching tree." Throughout the history of sport, we see a number of coaches who have been trained by other great coaches, continuing each legacy to form an incredible tree. Bob Knight, Pat Summitt, Knute Rockne, Tommy Lasorda—all have great coaching trees because at one time or another, they committed themselves to being taught and gained the knowledge they needed to give to others. In basketball, for example, Dean Smith's coaching had many branches that grew out to the high school, college and professional ranks. And these branches included coaches who have and still are following in his footsteps.

Today's verse gives us the wisdom that we need to be effective coaches as we commit ourselves to instruction and to listening to and applying the words of knowledge. What's even more exciting, though, is realizing that we can have a greater influence beyond our sport! If we follow Jesus Christ, we can have an eternal impact. When we spread God's Word to the unbelieving world, we have the opportunity to grow branches that bear fruit for His kingdom.

Of course, this happens only as we commit to gaining godly instruction and growing deep roots in His knowledge, wisdom and love. It comes when we are firmly planted in the truth of another tree: the tree on which Christ sacrificed His life for our sins and gave us the good news of eternal hope! As we stay anchored in Him, we can be transplanted and grow new branches for His sake.

Just as we know coaches whose tree of influence is great, we also know that Christ desires nothing less for us. He wants us to come to Him daily and learn from Him, gaining the heavenly knowledge that we need to lead others to the Tree of Life! —*Jere Johnson*

1. Whose example are you following or learning from right now?

2. Who could you be instructing in the ways of Christ?

3. How can you start being more committed to gaining godly wisdom today?

Scripture: Proverbs 4:7; Colossians 3:16; Titus 2; James 1:5-8

Prayer: *Great is Your faithfulness, God, my Father. Knowledge of You is a Tree of Life for me today and every day! Amen.*

The Priceless Gift of Serving!

So if anyone purifies himself from these things, he will be a special instrument, set apart, useful to the Master, prepared for every good work.

2 TIMOTHY 2:21

Most people think that serving is the same as service, but I believe that there is a huge difference between the two. Service is something we pay for or something we might come to expect at a restaurant or at a gas station. But serving goes deeper. Serving deals with heart issues, involves sacrifice and meets real needs. We don't pay for serving, though it can be costly.

Christ did not come to give good service. He came to serve. Athletes are not required to give good service to their teammates, but Christian athletes are called to serve. Coaches who follow the greatest servant who ever lived also have the privilege of serving their teams, not just providing a service to them.

Christ desires that we become servants to our players, teammates, friends, families and communities. We are His instruments—His serving instruments! That might be hard to understand in a world where it seems everyone wants to be a leader, not a servant. But Jesus never told us to be leaders. Instead, He invited us to be servants, and He did so at a cost. He served us with the ultimate sacrifice—His life—so that we might come into a right relationship with our holy God!

That's the most priceless news we could ever hear. It's why leadership camps sponsored by the Fellowship of Christian Athletes are really servant camps; their one goal is for the young people who attend to meet the most amazing servant ever to walk the earth, Jesus Christ. If we ever hope to lead, we must learn to serve. How? From the One who came to serve that we might follow in His steps!
—Dan Britton

1. How can you serve your players, colleagues, friends and family members?

2. Who are some servant-leaders who have impacted your life?

3. How has God gifted you to serve? How has He set you apart?

Scripture: Ephesians 2:10

Prayer: *Thank You, Lord of the Universe, for sending Jesus Christ to love and to serve the world so that my life might become an extension of His gift of service to others! Amen.*

Serving deals with heart issues, involves sacrifice and meets real needs. We don't pay for serving, though it can be costly.

> You yourselves are our letter, written on
> our hearts, recognized and read by everyone,
> since it is plain that you are Christ's letter,
> produced by us, not written with ink but with
> the Spirit of the living God; not on stone tablets
> but on tablets that are hearts of flesh.
>
> 2 CORINTHIANS 3:2-3

One of my favorite childhood memories came on my eleventh birthday, March 15, 1972. I received a gift that would set me head and shoulders above everyone else in the neighborhood. It was something that would make me the envy of all my friends.

I received the coolest bicycle in the world—a real "big boy" bike. I'm telling you, it was so shiny and bright. It had a white frame with a blue glitter banana seat, blue glitter handles and tassels. It did indeed make me the envy of all my friends. That bike made me the coolest kid in the neighborhood.

The coolest thing about that bike was its blue tires. I was the only kid in town who could lay blue streaks on the sidewalk. The other kids could only lay black. We'd all line up together, race down the sidewalk and then slam on our brakes to see who could leave the longest mark. Mine was always blue. If there was a blue streak on the sidewalk, you'd know I had been there. I had left my mark, and everybody knew whose it was.

As Christian coaches, God calls us to leave marks on the places that we've been. We are called to influence others for Christ. Whether it is at work, at home or around the neighborhood, God calls us to live a life that reaches out to others and glorifies Him.

We are called to "leave our marks" on our athletes, and that mark needs to look as much like Christ as possible. So today, ask yourself, What kind of mark are you leaving? —*Brad Holloway*

1. What opportunities do you have today to leave your mark?

2. What impact does it have on athletes and coaches when they see the mark that you have left behind?

3. Can you say that the mark you are leaving resembles Christ?

Scripture: Acts 9:36-42; 1 Corinthians 2:1-5; Philippians 1:13

Prayer: *Lord, help me to realize that pointing others to You is the highest calling that I have. Help me to see that the greatest goal I can reach is to make an eternal impact on the lives of those whom You have put in my path. Amen.*

Off-Season Work

The son who gathers during summer is prudent; the son who sleeps during harvest is disgraceful.

PROVERBS 10:5

When I was a coach, one of my biggest challenges was helping my athletes understand that improvement happened in the off-season. Each year, I got the same song and dance about how they had worked hard during the season and needed time off in the summer. Yet I knew that a strong work ethic was crucial to my athletes' success. Those who "kept at it" in season and out were better off in the end.

In Proverbs 10, Solomon teaches us about a wise young person who worked hard all summer and did not waste time. Apparently, the young people in Solomon's day also needed to make the most of their opportunities, though they didn't have as many of today's distractions, like video games and cable TV.

It's not easy helping young athletes understand the year-round effort required to improve their game. So I'm encouraged whenever I see young people shooting baskets, playing catch or riding bikes rather than sitting around.

Obviously, whatever our work—teaching, coaching, administering—we need to take it seriously. This also applies to our relationship with Christ. It takes disciplined time to get to know Him and grow closer to Him. Yet the more we do, the more we want to be with Him. Why?

Because we discover in Jesus Christ not only the standard for our work ethic but also the trustworthy God who loves us enough to sacrifice His life on the cross to bring us to Him. Through His Holy Spirit, He delights in working in us that which pleases Him (see Hebrews 13:21), shaping our character, directing our steps and using our gifts—professional or spiritual—for His purposes.

As we draw near to Him daily, wanting to hear His voice and learn His ways, we can't help but find ourselves eager to work toward the "harvest," in season or out! —*Jere Johnson*

1. What does your daily workout look like? Your daily devotional time with God?

2. Are you content with where you are as a coach? As a Christian?

3. How can you start today to work for Christ's glory?

Scripture: Proverbs 10; Matthew 25:14-30; Hebrews 6:10-12

Prayer: *Thank You, Lord God, that in You I live and move and have my being! Help me to work today with the grace You provide in Christ! Amen.*

Teach a youth about the way he should go;
even when he is old he will not depart from it.

PROVERBS 22:6

Coaches are always looking for the winning edge. We continually explore new techniques or systems to improve our programs. We go to clinics, conferences and seminars to learn how it should be done. Of course, no one coach is successful 100 percent of the time. But I know one coach who always did it right.

The Master Coach personally selected His own team. He poured His life into a team of 12, worked with them for 3 years, and then sent them out to teach and prepare others for future good work. In fact, He instilled lasting leadership skills among His team in the following five ways: (1) He empowered them—He gave them confidence to be bold in Him. (2) He equpped them—He prepared them for future ministry for Him. (3) He educated them—He gave wisdom to direct others to Him. (4) He edified them—He built them up in the Word to share about Him. (5) He encouraged them—He blessed their lives by a relationship with Him.

Jesus was—and is—the Master Coach. His teachings are the only foolproof way to find meaning, peace and victory in life. Because the young people in our programs deserve the best, we can help them learn from the best coach there ever was or will be—Jesus Christ. He is the one who poured His life out on the cross in the ultimate act of leadership: service.

Would your players say that you empower, equip, educate, edify and encourage them daily? If you give them Jesus, you've done all five. Remember, we have the opportunity to teach players more than just their sport; we can also leave a legacy by living the leadership we believe in, by living Jesus Christ daily! Only He will last forever with them! —*Jere Johnson*

1. What lesson or skill has remained with you from a coach that you had?

2. What practical steps can you take today to lead your players in the way Christ led His followers and to build a lasting legacy of leadership?

3. How can you help your players learn from the Master Coach?

Scripture: Mark 12:30; John 14:6; Ephesians 6:4

Prayer: *Thank You, Lord Jesus, that You have empowered me with Your Spirit so that I may equip and encourage others for Your work. Amen.*

The Power of Joy

At the dedication of the wall of Jerusalem, they sent for the Levites wherever they lived and brought them to Jerusalem to celebrate the joyous dedication with thanksgiving and singing accompanied by cymbals, harps, and lyres.

NEHEMIAH 12:27

A large crowd gathered for the memorial service of Coach Whitson, a much-loved junior high coach who had been at the same school for 17 years. Several former players spoke of his impact on their lives, describing him as happy and joyful.

Those close to him knew what they were talking about, because Coach Whitson understood what it meant to offer thanksgiving and praise to God regardless of the circumstances. He walked in worship, even when the circumstances were not happy. Though he had had his share of pain, his focus on thanksgiving gave him a joy that touched many lives.

Under the leadership of Nehemiah and others, the Jews returned to Jerusalem. They rebuilt the city wall and set up a secure government. They celebrated all that had occurred with gladness and joy. Why?

Because their eyes were on the Lord and what He had done for them. How do we know? Because they celebrated with hymns of thanksgiving. Nehemiah 12:43 says that all the people joined in and that their rejoicing was "heard from afar"—not their *singing*, but their *rejoicing*.

Focusing on God's goodness throughout the day is what I call "walking in worship," or "walking in joy." When we do this, people notice! Noah Webster, a committed Christian, offered this definition of "joy" in his 1828 *American Dictionary of the English Language*: "The passion or emotion excited by the acquisition or expectation of good."

All we have acquired from God through Jesus Christ's life and death is good. Joy is ours when we look to Him in thanksgiving or in expectation of what He has in store for us. That's why I call it walking in worship. Few things are more powerful than Christian joy! —*Bill Burnett*

1. On what occasions have you experienced joy?

2. Does the world see joy in you? Are they drawn to Christ because of your joy?

3. Do you bring joy to those you lead?

Scripture: Nehemiah 12:27-43; Job 8:19-22; John 15:1-11

Prayer: *Gracious God, I have much to be thankful for today. As I reflect on Your many gifts in my life, may others see Your joy! Amen.*

Therefore, fear the Lord and worship Him in sincerity and truth. Get rid of the gods your ancestors worshiped beyond the Euphrates River and in Egypt, and worship the Lord.

JOSHUA 24:14

Not long ago, I stopped in a nearby town for coffee. When I went to wash my hands, I noticed the shiny new hand dryer on the restroom wall with the words "Feel the Power" printed on it.

I pushed the button and got a blast of hot air! It was like one of those huge dryers from the car wash had been compacted into a tiny hand dryer. Now, whenever someone mentions that town, I think of that hand dryer, a silly reminder of my experience there!

Sometimes I wonder how I'll be remembered as a coach. When someone mentions my coaching career, will they note the wins and losses, the calls I made or failed to make? Or will they remember how I served and acted as a coach?

When people talk about Joshua, the first thing I remember is that he chose to serve the Lord when he could have pursued any other way to live. Joshua's life and leadership clearly reflected what he believed and whom he followed: God. He knew that humans are made to worship and that if we do not worship the one true God, we will worship another.

Thankfully, God sent His Son, Jesus Christ, to lead us to Himself and then gave us His Holy Spirit to fill us with the power we need to believe! When we submit ourselves to His lordship, our lives will reflect His contagious love and selfless power.

People might never know just who is behind our actions, but they will remember that something about our lives was different! They might forget records and scores, but they will not forget our Christlike actions. —*Rex Stump*

1. Which do you remember most: past scores, records or people?

2. What do you remember about one of your coaches or teammates?

3. How do you want to be remembered?

Scripture: Psalm 112; Ecclesiastes 2; Ezekiel 18:21-32; Ephesians 1:17-20

Prayer: *Lord, thank You that Your resurrection power is working in me to create a life that reminds others of You! Amen.*

Consumed by a Desire to Serve

Based on the gift they have received, everyone should use it to serve others, as good managers of the varied grace of God. If anyone speaks, his speech should be like the oracles of God; if anyone serves, his service should be from the strength God provides, so that in everything God may be glorified through Jesus Christ. To Him belong the glory and the power forever and ever. Amen.

1 PETER 4:10-1.1

As Christian competitors, we realize that God has called us to serve. But do we understand that we should be consumed to serve? Is there a consuming fire that burns in us to serve others around us who are hurting and to help those who need to experience the love of Christ through us?

We serve because the ultimate purpose of serving is to glorify Christ. Rick Warren said, "We serve God by serving others. The world defines greatness in terms of power, possessions, prestige, and position. . . . In our self-serving culture with its me-first mentality, acting like a servant is not a popular concept."[9] In the athletic world, everyone struggles to some degree with the "me first" mentality. We buy into the lie that we are better than others because of our giftedness in athletics. So are we consumed with self or consumed with serving?

When serving, we need to have intentionality (*plan it!*), intensity (*seize it!*) and intimacy (*feel it!*). The passion for serving must come from the heart. Samuel Chadwick said it best: "Spirit filled souls are ablaze for God. They love with a love that glows. They serve with a faith that kindles. They serve with a devotion that consumes. They hate sin with fierceness that burns. They rejoice with a joy that radiates. Love is perfected in the fire of God."[10]

On and off the field of competition, we need to be radical about serving. Can you imagine if thousands of coaches and athletes across the country got passionate about serving their teams? Why shouldn't that revolution begin with you? —*Dan Britton*

1. Why is it hard to be passionate about serving? What gets in the way?

2. What part of your life reflects the "me first" mentality? Identify it, confess it, and ask for forgiveness.

3. Will you be one of the thousands who are passionate about serving? If so, what is one practical way you can serve your team today?

Scripture: Jude 1:24-25

Prayer: *Jesus, this serving thing is hard. I struggle daily with the "me first" mentality. I confess my selfishness before You. Help me to see with spiritual eyes the ways I can serve my team. I want to be one who is consumed to serve. Amen.*

**After Moses came back, He summoned the
elders of the people, and put before them all these
words that the Lord had commanded him.**

EXODUS 19:7

Coaches work hard to get the job done for their programs, but the head coach spends even more time in preparation for his or her meetings with staff in order to plan for the year ahead. And it's not just the season preparations that need to be done—preseason, post-season and summer workouts also need to be considered. The head coach must think of everyone in the program and then blend everyone together for the success of the next year.

Moses had quite a team. After patiently dealing with Pharaoh, the Israelites finally were given the freedom to go with their head coach and leader, Moses. Moses listened to and followed God in order to lead his team through their journey. Though his team grumbled many times, Moses convinced them to stick with the plan. Moses would go and speak with God and then come back and meet with his "assistant coaches" (elders or tribal leaders) and present to them God's game plan for the day or week. The Israelites responded to God's plan through Moses by saying that they would do all the Lord had asked of them. However, Moses' team did not always follow the plan. They relied on their own selfish desires and disobeyed. Yes, Moses had quite a team.

As coaches, we need to stick with the plan even in tough times. If we endure, we may reach our ultimate goal one day. As believers, it is important that we follow God's game plan for our lives. Just because our Coach, Jesus Christ, is not among us in person today, His Spirit can lead and guide us, helping us to stick with the plan. He also equips us to assist Him in carrying out His game plan for others. This flawless game plan is the only one that you will ever need! —*Jere Johnson*

1. Is your game plan prepared, planned and presented to your staff before you share it with your team?

2. Do you know God's game plan for your life?

3. How can you start to implement God's plan for your life today?

Scripture: Exodus 21; Proverbs 3:5-6

Prayer: *Lord, please show me where I need to adjust my game plan to fit Yours. I pray this in Jesus' name, amen.*

Free to Be Our Best

Whatever you do, do it enthusiastically,
as something done for the Lord, and not for
men, since you know that you will receive an
inheritance from the Lord as a reward.
COLOSSIANS 3:23-24

As coaches and athletes, we put all of our hearts, bodies and emotions into our endeavors. We're instructed to give it all we've got, and as we do, we begin to understand what Paul was saying to the Colossian Christians.

In the second part of this passage, Paul communicates what could happen if our efforts were fully focused on honoring God, rather than man. But that's not easy in today's performance-based and self-centered society, in which we attach our personal value, worth and dignity to our performance. The more we work to gain notoriety or to impress others, the more we find that we are not free at all to be the people we were created by God to be. In fact, the pressure to win that most of us feel, as well as the fear we have of failing, only guarantees a roller-coaster performance, never our best.

The good news is that Paul experienced firsthand one of the most freeing principles of the Christian life: that what we do is *not* who we are! He wanted us to understand that our value is based solely on what Jesus did for us on the cross, not on what we can do through our own effort. When we understand and accept the reality of Christ's offering, we are *free* to be who we were intended to be. And when we experience His unconditional and sacrificial love (as Paul did), our hearts only want to seek and honor God more!

Knowing that our ability comes from God and that He loves us regardless of how we perform actually eliminates the need we have to perform for others. It frees us from allowing their opinions to control our decisions, because we're too busy putting our whole heart into our effort for the Lord! —*Phil Jones*

1. What, or who, gives you self-worth or value?

2. How can you keep your players from believing the lie that they are what they do?

3. How can you be free to coach with enthusiasm for the Lord, not for others?

Scripture: Psalm 37:1-6; Matthew 6:5-8,26-34

Prayer: *Yes, Lord, help me to work enthusiastically today for You and with You so that others might know the riches of Your love! Amen.*

Commit your way to the Lord; trust in Him, and He will act, making your righteousness shine like the dawn, your justice like the noonday.

Psalm 37:5-6

Rejoice always! Pray constantly.
Give thanks in everything, for this is God's
will for you in Christ Jesus.
1 THESSALONIANS 5:16-18

If you were to list the qualities of the people you most admire, a thankful attitude would probably be at the top of the list. Attitude will make or break a person. In his book *Developing the Leader Within You*, John Maxwell says this concerning attitude:

> The disposition of a leader is important because it will influence the way the followers think and feel. Great leaders understand that the right attitude will set the right atmosphere, which enables the right responses from others.[11]

Attitude is always a choice. You may not be able to control circumstances, but you can control how you react to those circumstances. Knowing that God is in control should make a difference in one's attitude. In fact, 1 Thessalonians 5:16-18 implies that our trust in God is directly linked to our attitude. One of the most difficult disciplines in life is the discipline of thankfulness—taking time to thank God for the team, children and spouse He has given you; taking time to count your blessings and adjust your attitude.

Paying bills used to be a pain in my side. When I would finish, I would be like an angry bear. (Can you relate? Most coaches can identify with the bumper sticker that reads "My take home pay won't even take me home!") Interest, taxes and high costs for services all made me angry. Then, one day as I was writing out the checks, the Lord spoke to my heart about being thankful that He had provided the income to pay those bills. Since that day, as I write each check, I have thanked God for His provision, and I am no longer like an angry bear when I finish. —*Al Schierbaum*

1. What are some blessings that God has given to you in the past year?

2. What attitudes bring glory to God?

3. How does your attitude create the right atmosphere for your team?

Scripture: Psalm 46:10; Matthew 5:14-16; Philippians 4:6-7; 1 Thessalonians 5:12-22

Prayer: *Father, thank You for the way You love me and want Your best for me. Thank You for the peace that surpasses all understanding.*

True Success

> The Lord answered her, "Martha, Martha, you are worried and upset about many things, but one thing is necessary. Mary has made the right choice, and it will not be taken away from her."
>
> LUKE 10:41-42

According to society's standards, a coach's status is based on his or her win-loss record. Unfortunately, a coach's personal worth is often tied into this same evaluation. The scoreboard is a clear-cut way to determine playoff selections, but it is a dangerous barometer for a coach to use as the measure of personal success.

Feeling down after a losing season, I sought out one of my coaching mentors to discuss my disappointment. He asked if I knew his record from the past season. I apologized that I hadn't followed his season. To my surprise, he informed me of his 11-1 record and a junior college bowl championship!

He then asked if I cared about him, since I hadn't followed his team's record during the past season. "I certainly do care about you!" I responded. My respect for him was based on who he was as a person, not his football success. "Then why are you in a funk because of last year's losing season?" he asked.

Jesus also provided a unique perspective on success through the story of Mary and Martha. While Martha was busy fulfilling the perceived demands of the moment, Mary sat listening to Jesus. Martha was upset by her sister's lack of help and asked Jesus to tell Mary to lend a hand. Jesus answered by pointing her to what mattered more than worldly accomplishments: a relationship with Him. That's why He came to Earth: to die a death we should have died so that we could have new life in Him!

The rewards of a winning record can be taken away by one "bad" year. But true success—an intimate relationship with God through Jesus—can never be taken away, because of the cross. We all are successful if we are in Christ! —*Victor Santa Cruz*

1. How do you respond to a loss?

2. Does the daily grind leave you without joy?

3. How do you define success?

Scripture: Ecclesiastes 2:4-11; Matthew 6:25-34; Mark 10:17-31

Prayer: *Lord, I pray that You will tear down the idols of success that I trust in. Renew my intimacy with You that I may fulfill my professional responsibilities with excellence and joy. You are my success! Amen.*

Endnotes

1. Reggie Miller, interview with David Brenner and Conrad Brunner, "Farewell Questions and Answers." http://www.nba.com/pacers/news/reggie_interview.html (accessed September 2005).

2. P. T. Forsyth, *The Soul of Prayer* (Vancouver, Canada: Regent College Publishing, 2002), n.p.

3. Jerry Bridges, *The Practice of Godliness* (Colorado Springs, CO: NavPress Publishing Group, 1996), n.p.

4. Oswald Chambers, *My Utmost for His Highest* (Grand Rapids, MI: Discovery House Publishers, 1992), n.p. Emphasis added.

5. Charitie L. Bancroft, "Before the Throne of God Above." http://www.cyberhymnal.org/htm/b/e/beforetg.htm (accessed September 2005).

6. Anna B. Warner, "Jesus Loves Me," *The Celebration Hymnal* (Nashville, TN: Word Music/Integrity Music), no. 185.

7. Lisette Hilton, "Auerbach's Celtics Played As a Team," *ESPN Classic Sportscentury Biography*. http://espn.go.com/classic/biography/s/auerbach_red.html (accessed September 2005).

8. Vartan Kupelian, "PGA Tour Would Benefit Greatly from Sorenstam Sequel," *The Detroit News Sports Insider*. http://www.detnews.com/2003/golf/0305/28/d01-173983.htm (accessed September 2005).

9. Rick Warren, *The Purpose-Driven Life: What on Earth Am I Here For?* (Grand Rapids, MI: Zondervan Publishing House), Day 33.

10. Samuel Chadwick, quoted on "WatchCry Quotes: Provoking Thoughts on Prayer, Revival and Missions," *Revival Resource Center*. http://www.watchword.org/fire_from_the_altar_of_prayer.htm (accessed October 2005).

11. John C. Maxwell, *Developing the Leader Within You* (Nashville, TN: Thomas Nelson Business, 2000), p. 98.

Thanks

Thanks from FCA to:

Donna Noonan, Bethany Hermes, Teri Wolfgang, Ashley Grosse, Jill Ewert and everyone who worked tirelessly to make this project happen.

To all the athletes and coaches who are:
Sharing Christ boldly;
Seeking Christ passionately;
Leading others faithfully;
and Loving others unconditionally.

To Bill Greig III, Roger Thompson, Steven Lawson, Mark Weising, Rob Williams and David Griffing at Regal Books.

To all FCA staff across the country who demonstrate integrity, serving, teamwork and excellence as they work to see the world impacted for Jesus Christ.

John Ausmus is a former college baseball coach and served as an FCA huddle coach for 10 years. Currently, he is a businessman in Garland, Texas, and an NCAA baseball umpire.

Cheryl Baird was an All-American volleyball player at Wheaton College in Wheaton, Illinois, and has been an assistant coach with junior track and in college volleyball. She and her family reside in Wheaton.

Dan Britton serves as the Senior Vice President of Ministries of FCA at the national headquarters in Kansas City, Missouri. In high school and college, Dan was a standout lacrosse player. Dan and his family reside in Overland Park, Kansas.

Jenny Burgins serves as the Rockmart High School girls' varsity soccer coach in Rockmart, Georgia. She has been actively involved in bringing high school athletes to Black Mountain FCA Camp in North Carolina. Jenny and her family live in Rockmart.

Bill Burnett is the FCA Director in Northwest Arkansas. Bill was an outstanding running back for the University of Arkansas and still holds the single-season and career scoring records for the Razorbacks.

Danny Burns is Manager of Online Ministry at FCA's national headquarters in Kansas City, Missouri. Danny served as a huddle leader and varsity distance runner at Northwest Missouri State University and has a passion for advancing the college ministry at FCA.

Josh Carter is the Area Director for North Central Illinois FCA. He is a former high school coach and teacher.

Alvin Cheng was a four-year tennis letterman at Eastern Kentucky University, where he currently serves as the assistant tennis coach. Alvin was a Buddhist when he came from Malaysia to attend college in the United States but received Christ during his freshman year.

Laura Crawford works at Kenneth Cooper Middle School in Oklahoma City, Oklahoma, where she teaches seventh-grade English and sponsors FCA, spirit committee and athletics.

Clay Elliot played pro baseball for five years in the Atlanta Braves organization. He is now the FCA Director for Santa Clara County in Northern California.

Jim Faulk is a former football and basketball coach and was an FCA huddle leader in the early 1980s. He currently serves on staff at FCA in San Antonio, Texas.

Lisa Fisher serves as assistant women's basketball coach at Washington State University in Pullman, Washington. She played collegiate basketball at Boise State University.

Charles Gee is an FCA staff member serving the Midlands South Carolina area. A former high school teacher and coach, Charles and his family reside in Columbia, South Carolina.

Debbie Haliday coaches middle school and high school girls' basketball at Hillcrest Christian School in Granada Hills, California. She attended UCLA where she was a member of both the women's softball and basketball teams. She is also Regional Camp Director for Southern California FCA. Debbie and her family live in Southern California.

Michael Hill has served as a football coach at both the college and high school levels. He is now the FCA Area Representative for Southeast Kansas and lives with his family in Winfield, Kansas.

Brad Holloway is an FCA huddle coach. He teaches and coaches football and wrestling at Union Grove Middle School in McDonough, Georgia.

Scott Jackson is a teacher and defensive coordinator for the football team at East Paulding High School in Dallas, Georgia. He was a walk-on member of the University of Georgia football team.

Phil Jones has coached in high school and college for 36 years and is now the head football coach at Shorter College in Rome, Georgia. Phil and his family live in Rome.

Jenny Johnson is a high school tennis coach and an adjunct faculty member of both Williamsburg Technical College and Coastal Carolina University. Jenny and her family reside in Lake City, South Carolina.

Jere Johnson is a former basketball coach for Indiana Wesleyan University, Oklahoma Wesleyan University and Lakeview Christian School. He currently serves as an FCA staff member in the greater Chicago area.

Susan Johnson is the head women's basketball coach at Georgetown College in Georgetown, Kentucky. She has also served as the women's tennis coach and as a professor of kinesiology and health studies.

Jo Kadlecek was the founding head coach for the women's soccer program at Colorado Christian University. She has been involved with FCA since 1984, when she was a high school girls' soccer and girls' basketball coach. Jo and her husband reside in Bradley Beach, New Jersey.

Larry Kerr has more than 20 years of coaching experience and serves as the defensive coordinator for the UCLA football team. Larry played football at San Jose State University.

Ken Kladnik is a certified athletic trainer and the head athletic trainer at Central Washington University in Ellensburg, Washington. He is also active in FCA as a huddle coach.

Donalyn Knight is a life management skills teacher at Seminole High School in Sanford, Florida. She has been involved with FCA for more than 30 years as a coach and huddle sponsor and has also served as the chaplain to the WNBA Orlando Miracle.

Roger Lipe is the Southern Illinois representative for the FCA and serves as the chaplain for the Southern Illinois University athletic teams. He is also the author of several devotional books. Roger and his family live in Carbondale, Illinois.

Chip Mehaffey is a mathematics teacher and coach of the boys' varsity basketball at Winchester Community High School in Winchester, Indiana.

Kathy Malone is a certified athletic trainer in a sports medicine clinic that serves several high schools in Indianapolis, Indiana. She is also an FCA volunteer and serves as chaplain for the WNBA's Indiana Fever.

Donna Miller is director of athletics at Mary Baldwin College in Staunton, Virginia. She previously coached intercollegiate tennis for 15 years with stints at Virginia Intermont College, Eastern Mennonite University and Mary Baldwin College.

Wayne Morrow is a former track coach who now serves as an FCA huddle leader at Grants Pass High School in Grants Pass, Oregon.

Lisa Phillips serves as the varsity softball coach at Bremen High School in Bremen, Georgia. She is also the school's FCA huddle coach.

Chanda Husser Rigby is the head women's basketball coach at Holmes Community College in Goodman, Mississippi, where she also serves as the FCA huddle coach.

Sue Ramsey is the head women's basketball coach and senior women's administrator at Ashland University in Ohio. Coach Ramsey enjoys the opportunities to share with others as a motivational speaker.

Victor Santa Cruz is the defensive coordinator and secondary coach for the football team at Azusa Pacific University in Azusa, California. Victor and his family reside in Glendora, California.

Al Schierbaum coached baseball at Dallas Baptist University for 11 years and has coached two summer touring teams. He currently serves as the Great Lakes Regional Director for FCA. He and his family reside in Streetsboro, Ohio.

Dr. Toby C. Schwartz is the head cross country/track and field coach at Whitworth College in Spokane, Washington. In nine seasons, Toby has been recognized eight times as coach of the year. He has coached more than 65 national qualifiers and 12 All-Americans, including a national champion in the women's 100 meter in 2004.

Joel Schuldheisz has been the athletics director at Concordia University-Portland, Oregon, for more than 20 years. Joel serves as the FCA huddle coach at the university. He and his family reside in Portland.

Jim Shapiro is the head football coach at King's High School in Seattle, Washington, and has served in this capacity for the last eight seasons. He played college football at Pacific Lutheran University, where in 1993 his team won the NAIA Division II national championship.

Bob "Ish" Smith currently serves as FCA Area Director for Southern Illinois. He coached college baseball for 18 years and has served as president of both the United States Baseball Federation and the International Baseball Association.

Eileen F. Sommi is a former field hockey coach.

Les Steckel spent 30 years coaching football at the high school, college and professional levels (his teams at the professional level reached two Super Bowls). He currently serves as president/CEO of FCA. Les and his wife, Chris, reside in Overland Park, Kansas.

Rex Stump currently serves as the Area Representative for the Buckeye Border (Ohio) FCA. He also coaches the girl's varsity volleyball and serves as the chaplain for the Defiance College football team. Rex and his family live in Wauseon, Ohio.

Scott Wade is an FCA area representative in Hampton Roads, Virginia. He also serves as a junior varsity football coach in his hometown of Yorktown, Virginia, where he lives with his family. Scott played football at Carson-Newman College in Jefferson City, Tennessee.

Amy Walz was the director of goalkeeping at Littleton United Soccer Club in Littleton, Colorado. She has coached competitive club, high school and college soccer, and currently makes her home in Southern California.

Bryan Wells serves as head football coach at Neuqua Valley High School in Naperville, Illinois. Bryan has coached for 19 years with stays in Georgia, Kansas and Illinois. Bryan and his family reside in Aurora, Illinois.

Michael Wiggins is the Senior Vice President, Chief Operating Officer for Lewis-Gale Clinic in Salem, Virginia. Michael is an avid runner and cyclist and competes in marathons, centuries and other endurance races.

Kathie Woods is in her twenty-fifth year of coaching volleyball and is the head coach at Clackamas Community College in Oregon City, Oregon. She is also the FCA huddle leader at her school and presently serves on an Oregon board for FCA.

"IMPACTING THE WORLD FOR CHRIST THROUGH SPORTS"

The Fellowship of Christian Athletes is touching millions of lives ... one heart at a time. Since 1954, the Fellowship of Christian Athletes has been challenging coaches and athletes on the professional, college, high school, junior high and youth levels to use the powerful medium of athletics to impact the world for Jesus Christ. FCA is the largest interdenominational, school-based, Christian sports ministry in America. FCA focuses on serving local communities by equipping, empowering and encouraging people to make a difference for Christ.

VISION

To see the world impacted for Jesus Christ
through the influence of athletes and coaches.

MISSION

To present to athletes and coaches and all whom they influence the challenge and adventure of receiving Jesus Christ as Savior and Lord, serving Him in their relationships and in the fellowship of the church.

MINISTRIES

The FCA Ministries encourage, equip and empower coaches and athletes on the professional, college, high school, junior high and youth levels to use the powerful medium of sports to impact their world for Jesus Christ.

The FCA Ministries are:
- **Coaches**
- **Campus**
- **Camp**
- **Community**

FUNDAMENTALS

SHARE Him Boldly
SEEK Him Passionately
LEAD Others Faithfully
LOVE Others Unconditionally

VALUES

Our relationships will demonstrate steadfast commitment to Jesus Christ and His Word through **Integrity, Serving, Teamwork and Excellence**.

Fellowship of Christian Athletes
8701 Leeds Road · Kansas City, MO 64129
www.fca.org · fca@fca.org · 1-800-289-0909

I am a Christian first and last.
I am created in the likeness of God Almighty to bring Him glory.
I am a member of Team Jesus Christ.
I wear the colors of the cross.

I am a Competitor now and forever.
I am made to strive, to strain, to stretch and to succeed in the arena of competition.
I am a Christian Competitor and as such, I face my challenger with the face of Christ.

I do not trust in myself.
I do not boast in my abilities or believe in my own strength.
I rely solely on the power of God.
I compete for the pleasure of my Heavenly Father, the honor
of Christ and the reputation of the Holy Spirit.

My attitude on and off the field is above reproach—my conduct beyond criticism.
Whether I am preparing, practicing or playing,
I submit to God's authority and those He has put over me.
I respect my coaches, officials, teammates, and competitors out of respect for the Lord.

My body is the temple of Jesus Christ.
I protect it from within and without.
Nothing enters my body that does not honor the Living God.
My sweat is an offering to my Master. My soreness is a sacrifice to my Savior.

I give my all—all the time.
I do not give up. I do not give in. I do not give out.
I am the Lord's warrior—a competitor by conviction and a disciple of determination.
I am confident beyond reason because my confidence lies in Christ.
The results of my effort must result in His glory.

Let the competition begin.
Let the glory be God's.

Sign the Creed
Go to *www.fca.org*

COMPETITORS for CHRIST

THE COACH'S MANDATE

Pray as though nothing of eternal value is going
to happen in my athletes' lives unless God does it.

Prepare each practice and game as giving "my utmost for His highest."

Seek not to be served by my athletes for personal gain, but seek
to serve them as Christ served the church.

Be satisfied not with producing a good record, but with producing good athletes.

Attend carefully to my private and public walk with God, knowing that the
athlete will never rise to a standard higher than that being lived by the coach.

Exalt Christ in my coaching, trusting the Lord will then draw athletes to Himself.

Desire to have a growing hunger for God's Word, for personal
obedience, for fruit of the spirit and for saltiness in competition.

Depend solely upon God for transformation—one athlete at a time.

Preach Christ's word in a Christ-like demeanor, on and off the field of competition.

Recognize that it is impossible to bring glory to both myself
and Christ at the same time.

Allow my coaching to exude the fruit of the Spirit,
thus producing Christ-like athletes.

Trust God to produce in my athletes His chosen purposes,
regardless of whether the wins are readily visible.

Coach with humble gratitude, as one privileged to be God's coach.

COMPETITORS for CHRIST

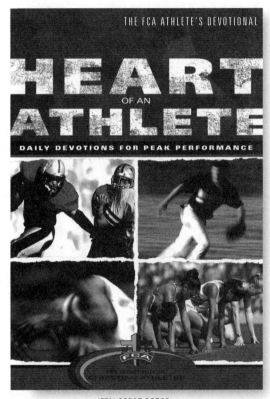

Go One-on-One with Sports Legends

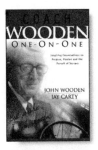
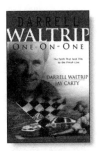
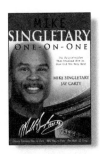
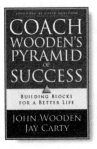
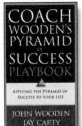